■ はしがき ■

　本書は，第一学習社発行の英語教科書「CREATIVE English Communication III」に完全準拠したワークブックです。見開き 2 ページで，教科書本文を使って「聞く」「読む」「話す（やり取り）」「話す（発表）」「書く」の 4 技能 5 領域の力を育成する問題をバランスよく用意しました。

■ 本書の構成と利用法 ■

JN102748

本文，Activity Plus のページ

教科書本文

・新出単語を太字で示しました。

・意味のまとまりごとにスラッシュを入れました。ここで示した意味のまとまりや，英語の強弱のリズム，イントネーションなどに注意して，本文を流暢に音読できるようにしましょう。付属のスピーキング・トレーナーを使って，自分の発話を後から確認できます。発話の流暢さ（1 分あたりの発話語数：words per minute）を算出する計算式を，本書巻末にまとめて掲載しています。

📖 Reading

・大学入学共通テストなどの形式に対応した，本文の内容理解問題です。

🔍 Vocabulary & Grammar

・英検®や GTEC®の形式に対応した，新出単語や新出表現，文法事項，重要語句についての問題です。

🎧 Listening

・本文内容やテーマに関連した短い英文を聞いて答える問題です。

・Activity Plus では，本文内容やテーマに関連したやや長い英文を聞いて答える問題を収録しています。

・🔘 は別売の音声 CD のトラック番号を示します。二次元コードを読み取って，音声を PC やスマートフォンなどから聞くこともできます。

💬 Interaction

・本文内容やテーマに関連した会話を聞いて，最後の発話に対して自分の考えなどを応答し，やり取りを完成させる活動です。

・付属のスピーキング・トレーナーを使って，自分の発話を後から確認することができます。

💬 Production (Speak)　　✏️ Production (Write)

・本文内容やテーマに関連した，自分自身に関する質問や，考えや意見を問う質問に話したり書いたりして答える表現活動です。

◆「知識・技能」や「思考力・判断力・表現力」を養成することを意識し，設問ごとに主に対応する観点を示しました。

◆ライティング，スピーキング問題を自分で採点できるようにしています。

　別冊『解答・解説集』の「ルーブリック評価表」（ある観点における学習の到達度を判断する基準）を用いて，自分の記述内容や発話内容が採点できます。

CONTENTS

CAN-DO List
知識・技能

❏🔊強弱のリズムを理解して音読することができる。

❏🔉分詞構文の否定形，語・連語・慣用表現について理解を深め，これらを適切に活用することができる。
❏🔊強弱のリズムを理解して音読することができる。

❏🔉無生物主語や，語・連語・慣用表現について理解を深め，これらを適切に活用することができる。
❏🔊強弱のリズムを理解して音読することができる。

❏🔉進行形の受け身や，語・連語・慣用表現について理解を深め，これらを適切に活用することができる。
❏🔊イントネーションを理解して音読することができる。

❏🔉語・連語・慣用表現について理解を深め，これらを適切に活用することができる。
❏🔊イントネーションを理解して音読することができる。

❏🔉語・連語・慣用表現について理解を深め，これらを適切に活用することができる。
❏🔊イントネーションを理解して音読することができる。

❏🔉語・連語・慣用表現について理解を深め，これらを適切に活用することができる。
❏🔊音の変化を理解して音読することができる。

❏🔉語・連語・慣用表現について理解を深め，これらを適切に活用することができる。
❏🔊音の変化を理解して音読することができる。

❏🔉形容詞で始まる分詞構文や，語・連語・慣用表現について理解を深め，これらを適切に活用することができる。
❏🔊音の変化を理解して音読することができる。

❏🔉if ... 以外が条件を表す仮定法や，語・連語・慣用表現について理解を深め，これらを適切に活用することができる。
❏🔊シャドーイングをすることができる。

❏🔉否定語を含まない否定や，語・連語・慣用表現について理解を深め，これらを適切に活用することができる。
❏🔊シャドーイングをすることができる。

❏🔉語・連語・慣用表現について理解を深め，これらを適切に活用することができる。
❏🔊シャドーイングをすることができる。

思考力・判断力・表現力

- ☐ 📖 短めの英文を読んで的確に理解し，その内容を整理することができる。
- ☐ 🎧 本文内容に関連する英文を聞いて，必要な情報を把握することができる。
- ☐ ✐ 本文内容に関連するテーマについて，自分の考えを書いて伝えることができる。

- ☐ 📖 高速鉄道の発達について的確に理解し，その内容を整理することができる。
- ☐ 🎧 鉄道に関する英文を聞いて，必要な情報を把握することができる。
- ☐ 💬 鉄道や交通機関について，適切に情報や考えを伝え合うことができる。
- ☐ 😊 新幹線について，自分の考えを話して伝えることができる。
- ☐ ✐ 技術革新について，情報や考えを書いて伝えることができる。

- ☐ 📖 世界の水問題と井戸掘り技術について的確に理解し，その内容を整理することができる。
- ☐ 🎧 水問題やNPOに関する英文を聞いて，必要な情報を把握することができる。
- ☐ 💬 水問題や井戸水について，適切に情報や考えを伝え合うことができる。
- ☐ 😊 飲料水について，自分の考えを話して伝えることができる。
- ☐ ✐ 途上国支援や課題解決について，情報や考えを書いて伝えることができる。

- ☐ 📖 アスリートの社会的なメッセージについて的確に理解し，その内容を整理することができる。
- ☐ 🎧 アスリートや社会に関する英文を聞いて，必要な情報を把握することができる。
- ☐ 💬 アスリートや文化について，適切に情報や考えを伝え合うことができる。
- ☐ 😊 スポーツについて，情報を話して伝えることができる。
- ☐ ✐ 差別について，情報や考えを書いて伝えることができる。

- ☐ 📖 赤ちゃんの言語習得について的確に理解し，その内容を整理することができる。
- ☐ 🎧 赤ちゃんや言語に関する英文を聞いて，必要な情報を把握することができる。
- ☐ 💬 言語習得について，適切に情報や考えを伝え合うことができる。
- ☐ 😊 教育について，自分の考えを話して伝えることができる。
- ☐ ✐ コミュニケーションについて，情報や考えを書いて伝えることができる。

- ☐ 📖 社会のデジタル化について的確に理解し，その内容を整理することができる。
- ☐ 🎧 デジタル化に関する英文を聞いて，必要な情報を把握することができる。
- ☐ 💬 デジタル化や文化について，適切に情報や考えを伝え合うことができる。
- ☐ 😊 デジタル化について，自分の考えを話して伝えることができる。
- ☐ ✐ デジタル化について，情報や考えを書いて伝えることができる。

- ☐ 📖 人類と病気の戦いの歴史について的確に理解し，その内容を整理することができる。
- ☐ 🎧 感染症や衛生環境に関する英文を聞いて，必要な情報を把握することができる。
- ☐ 💬 病気や医学について，適切に情報や考えを伝え合うことができる。
- ☐ 😊 リモートワークについて，情報を話して伝えることができる。
- ☐ ✐ 感染症について，情報や考えを書いて伝えることができる。

- ☐ 📖 スポーツ栄養について的確に理解し，その内容を整理することができる。
- ☐ 🎧 スポーツや食事に関する英文を聞いて，必要な情報を把握することができる。
- ☐ 💬 スポーツや栄養について適切に情報や考えを伝え合うことができる。
- ☐ 😊 スポーツについて，自分の考えを話して伝えることができる。
- ☐ ✐ 健康や栄養について，情報や考えを書いて伝えることができる。

- ☐ 📖 橋の構造と役割について的確に理解し，その内容を整理することができる。
- ☐ 🎧 橋や建築に関する英文を聞いて，必要な情報を把握することができる。
- ☐ 💬 橋や記念日について，適切に情報や考えを伝え合うことができる。
- ☐ 😊 古代文明について，自分の考えを話して伝えることができる。
- ☐ ✐ 橋やランドマークについて，情報や考えを書いて伝えることができる。

- ☐ 📖 ギンズバーグ判事の生涯について的確に理解し，その内容を整理することができる。
- ☐ 🎧 学習や学校に関する英文を聞いて，必要な情報を把握することができる。
- ☐ 💬 偉人や教育について，適切に情報や考えを伝え合うことができる。
- ☐ 😊 卒業スピーチについて，自分の考えを話して伝えることができる。
- ☐ ✐ 男女平等について，情報や考えを書いて伝えることができる。

- ☐ 📖 三代達也さんの生き方について的確に理解し，その内容を整理することができる。
- ☐ 🎧 障害ややさしさに関する英文を聞いて，必要な情報を把握することができる。
- ☐ 💬 生活や人生について，適切に情報や考えを伝え合うことができる。
- ☐ 😊 バリアフリーについて，自分の考えを話して伝えることができる。
- ☐ ✐ 生活や人生について，情報や考えを書いて伝えることができる。

- ☐ 📖 ストーリーの展開を的確に理解し，その内容を整理することができる。
- ☐ ✐ 日常生活や自分の経験，物語登場人物の心情について，自分の考えを書いて伝えることができる。

Fully electric cars are increasing / around the world. // Before they came into the market, / hybrid cars had gained in popularity. //

It has been more than a quarter of a century / since the first consumer hybrid car made its debut / in 1997, / and there are an increasing number of hybrid cars / on the market / these days. // Hybrid means a **combination** / of two different things. // A hybrid car is one / that uses two different energy sources / to maximize **efficiency**. // The reason for its growing popularity is / that it has several advantages / over a **conventional** car / powered by **gasoline**. // For example, / hybrid cars produce less **emissions** / and use less gasoline / by making good use / of an engine / and an electric **motor**. // They use one of them / or both / depending on driving conditions. // When the gasoline engine needs power, / it also uses an electric motor / so that it uses less gasoline. // On the other hand, / when the car is **braking**, / the energy is used / to charge the batteries. // As a result, / the longer the travel distance is, / the better the **fuel** efficiency tends to be. // In addition, / **taxes** on hybrid cars / have been cut / in recent years. // A hybrid car will **offer** greater economy, / tax benefits, / and fewer emissions / than a conventional car. // Therefore, / it is gaining strong support / from the public now. // (199 words)

🔊 **音読しよう**　　　　　　　　　　　　　　　　　　　　スピーキング・トレーナー

Practice 1　スラッシュ位置で文を区切って読んでみよう ☐
Practice 2　英語の強弱のリズムに注意して読んでみよう ☐
TRY!　　　2分以内に本文全体を音読しよう ☐

📖 **Reading**　本文の内容を読んで理解しよう【知識・技能】【思考力・判断力・表現力】　　共通テスト

Make the correct choice to complete each sentence or answer each question. (各6点)

1. The author ☐ .
   ① describes the features of hybrid cars
   ② has his own hybrid car
   ③ recommends buying a hybrid car rather than a gasoline car
   ④ states that hybrid cars are better than electric cars

2. Which of the following is **not** an appropriate advantage of hybrid cars? ☐
   ① Environmental performance.
   ② Low taxes.
   ③ Fuel efficiency.
   ④ Popularity.

🔍 Vocabulary　重要表現について理解しよう【知識】　　英検® GTEC®

Make the correct choice to complete each sentence. (各3点)

1. A pizza with pepperoni and mushrooms is an example of a (　　　) of toppings.
   ① combination　　② intersection　　③ subset　　④ union

2. Using a computer program can increase (　　　) in data analysis.
   ① complexity　　② efficiency　　③ redundancy　　④ simplicity

3. Cars produce harmful (　　　) that can contribute to air pollution and climate change.
   ① emissions　　② engines　　③ fuels　　④ transmissions

4. (　　　) is necessary for most vehicles to operate.
   ① A charger　　② Gasoline　　③ Hydrogen　　④ Water

5. Many people enjoy coffee in the morning. (　　　), others prefer tea.
   ① As a result　　　　　　② In addition
   ③ On the other hand　　④ Therefore

6. I studied hard for my exam. (　　　), I got a good grade.
   ① As a result　　　　　　② In addition
   ③ On the other hand　　④ Surprisingly

7. I went to the store to buy milk. (　　　), I bought some bread.
   ① As a result　　　　　　② In addition
   ③ On the other hand　　④ Therefore

✏️ Production (Write)　自分の考えを書いて伝えよう【思考力・判断力・表現力】

Write your answer to the following question. (7点)

Would you like to buy a hybrid or electric car even if the price is higher?

アドバイス　値段の高さというデメリットに対してメリットの方が大きいかどうか，考えてみよう。

A　There is a perfectly good word / for "no" / in the Japanese language, / but it is seldom used. // "Yes," / on the other hand, / is heard / all the time. // This does not mean, / however, / that the Japanese do not say "no." // In fact, / they say it / quite often, / even if what they have said sounds like "yes" / to **newcomers**. //

For many generations / the Japanese were conditioned / to avoid **blunt responses** / and **confrontations** / of any kind. // Since "no" is often **confrontational**, / the Japanese do not like / to come right out / and say it. //

The Japanese have also been almost as uncomfortable with "yes" / as they have been with "no." // "Yes" could, / and often did, / lead to new **commitments** and responsibilities. // As a result, / "yes" **gradually** came to be **synonymous** / with "Yes, / I heard you" / or "Yes, / I am listening," / **ceasing** to mean / "Yes, I agree with you." //

Thus / it happened / in Japan / that the use of "yes" and "no" / became very subtle, / requiring the **hearer** / to be **exceptionally** skilled / in interpreting / what the speaker meant. // The main reason for this / was the **overriding** need / to maintain harmony, / and the importance of **self-preservation**. //

B　Children / in developing countries work / for a variety of reasons; / the most common reason / is poverty. // Children work / so that they and their families can survive. // Though these children are not paid well, / their families are so poor / that they still serve / as major **contributors** / to family income. // For instance, / children in poor families / in **Paraguay** / contribute almost 25 percent / of the total household income. //

In developing countries, / **rural**-to-**urban migration** is another cause of child **labor**. // In the last 40 years, / more and more people have **migrated** / from the country / to the city. // In 1950, / just 17 percent of the population / of the developing world / lived in urban areas. // This figure increased / to 40 percent / by the year 2000. // It will probably reach 57 percent / by the year 2030. // Poor families / who move to the cities / usually do not find enough work. // Moving to the cities forces families / into poverty, / and poverty forces parents / to send children / to work. //　(348 words)

🔊 **音読しよう**　　　　　　　　　　　　　　　　スピーキング・トレーナー

Practice 1　スラッシュ位置で文を区切って読んでみよう □
Practice 2　英語の強弱のリズムに注意して読んでみよう □
TRY!　　　　3分30秒以内に本文全体を音読しよう □

📖 Reading 本文の内容を読んで理解しよう【知識・技能】【思考力・判断力・表現力】 共通テスト

Make the correct choice to complete each sentence or answer each question. (各6点)

1. According to Text A, Japanese people [＿＿＿].

   ① often express the meaning of "no" without using the word "no"

   ② often mistake the meaning of "yes" and "no"

   ③ tend not to say "no" to foreigners　　④ use the word "no" quite often

2. According to Text B, what impact does rural-to-urban migration typically have on families in developing countries? [＿＿＿]

   ① It has no impact on their economic situation.

   ② It helps them find better-paying jobs.

   ③ It often leads to poverty.　　④ It reduces the need for children to work.

🔍 Vocabulary 重要表現について理解しよう【知識】 英検® GTEC®

Make the correct choice to complete each sentence. (各3点)

1. The company's (　　　) to the customer's complaint was prompt and professional.

   ① decision　　② obstacle　　③ resource　　④ response

2. The sun (　　　) sets in the west.

   ① gradually　　② occasionally　　③ suddenly　　④ tragically

3. Jane made a (　　　) to work out at the gym three times a week.

   ① commitment　　② hesitation　　③ law　　④ rejection

4. The weather forecast predicts rain; (　　　), we should bring an umbrella.

   ① meanwhile　　② nonetheless　　③ then　　④ therefore

5. The (　　　) required for the project was huge, but the results were worth it.

   ① labor　　② party　　③ vacation　　④ wastes

6. Every year, some birds (　　　) to warmer climates during the winter months.

   ① immigrate　　② lay eggs　　③ migrate　　④ nest

7. We have some common images of colors. (　　　), the color green represents nature.

   ① For instance　　② Furthermore　　③ In conclusion　　④ Otherwise

✐ Production (Write) 自分の考えを書いて伝えよう【思考力・判断力・表現力】

Write your answer to the following question. (7点)

   Do you have the personality to say "no" clearly to your friend?

   アドバイス 自分の性格を考え，その理由や補足を付け加えよう。

People have lived / with **domesticated** animals / for thousands of years. // Typical examples / include sheep, / goats, / pigs, / horses / and chickens, / but dogs have been around / with us / longer than any other animal. // Some scientists **argue** / that dogs started moving around / with humans / about 20,000 years ago. // This is probably / why many people believe / "a dog is human's best friend." // However, / it is actually said / that there are more cats / in Japan / than dogs nowadays. // Cats have also been domesticated / for a long time / since around 7,500 BC. //

Japan is sometimes described / as a country / in which pets **outnumber** children. // According to the Japan Pet Food **Association**, / there are about 18 million cats and dogs, / while there are just around 15 million children / under the age of 15. // This trend is likely to continue / in the future. // (135 words)

🔊 音読しよう

スピーキング・トレーナー

Practice 1　スラッシュ位置で文を区切って読んでみよう ☐
Practice 2　英語の強弱のリズムに注意して読んでみよう ☐
TRY!　　　　1分20秒以内に本文全体を音読しよう ☐

📖 **Reading**　本文の内容を読んで理解しよう【知識・技能】【思考力・判断力・表現力】　　共通テスト

Make the correct choice to answer each question. (各6点)

1. Which of the following is the **fact** you can tell from the text? ☐

   ① A dog is human's best friend because of the close relationship between humans and dogs.
   ② Dogs are indispensable animals for humans.
   ③ The Japan Pet Food Association publishes the number of cats and dogs in Japan.
   ④ The number of dogs and cats in Japan will continue to increase.

2. What information do we need to determine whether "This trend is likely to continue in the future" is true? ☐

   ① The current number of households that own pets.
   ② The estimated future figures for the number of children and pets in Japan.
   ③ The growth rate of pet shop sales.
   ④ The number of pets and children outside of Japan.

🔍 Vocabulary　重要表現について理解しよう【知識】　英検® GTEC®

Make the correct choice to complete each sentence. (各 4 点)

1. Dogs are one of the most common (　　　) animals and have been living with humans for thousands of years.
   ① domesticated ② endangered ③ sophisticated ④ wild

2. They often (　　　) over the best way to increase sales.
   ① agree ② argue ③ discuss ④ dispute

3. My failures far (　　　) my successes.
   ① cooperate ② discourage ③ outnumber ④ superior

4. The painter describes what he feels (　　　) it is.
   ① as ② in ③ so ④ to

5. The current fashion (　　　) leans toward vintage styles and retro clothing.
   ① absence ② excitement ③ invention ④ trend

✏️ Production（Write）　自分の考えを書いて伝えよう【思考力・判断力・表現力】

Write your answer to the following question. (8 点)

Do you agree with the statement "A dogs is a human's best friend"?

アドバイス　理由も付け加えよう。

You've heard / about a **policy** change / in your city. // You are reading / the discussions about the policy / in an online **forum**. //

Subject: / **Abolishment** of Community Buses //

To whom it may concern, /

I am posting / to ask you / to continue the service of community buses / between Sakura Village / and the city center. // I heard / that the city is going to **abolish** the service / next September. //

My parents are both over 80 years old, / living on their own / in the village. // They don't drive / and frequently use community buses / to go shopping / in the city center. // I know / the amount of money being made / on the buses / is declining, / but I believe / the service is essential / for older people / in the village / like my parents. // Although the number of people using the service / seems to have dropped / recently, / I believe / there is still a possibility / of an increase / in users / because the city's population is aging / fast. // I would like your **reconsideration**. //

Regards, /

Martin Jones //

Dear Martin, //

Thank you / for your **inquiry**. // It was actually a tough decision / for us / to abolish the community buses. // Due to a lack of financial sources, / however, / we had to carry out / a review of local services / as a whole / and look carefully / at the **unprofitable** ones, / including the community buses. // The number of bus users has dropped / by 39% / since 2010. // I'm sorry / to have to say it, / but **unless** we can expect / an increase / in users, / it will be difficult / to **withdraw** the decision / to abolish the buses. //

Thank you very much / for your understanding. //

Sincerely, /

Miho Yamaguchi //

City Planning **Division** // (246 words)

🔊 音読しよう   スピーキング・トレーナー
Practice 1   スラッシュ位置で文を区切って読んでみよう ☐
Practice 2   英語の強弱のリズムに注意して読んでみよう ☐
TRY!   2分30秒以内に本文全体を音読しよう ☐

🕮 **Reading**　本文の内容を読んで理解しよう【知識・技能】【思考力・判断力・表現力】　共通テスト

Make the correct choice to complete each sentence or answer each question. (各6点)

1. The city decided to abolish the community buses because ⬚.

① it had run out of budget　　② of the aging of the community

③ they were unprofitable　　④ they were not needed by passengers

2. Which of the following events could lead to the city withdrawing its decision to abolish community buses? ⬚

① An increase in the city's population

② Easing of the declining birth rate and aging population

③ Increased demand to withdraw the abolition of buses

④ Reduced congestion on the city's roads

🔎 **Vocabulary**　重要表現について理解しよう【知識】　英検® GTEC®

Make the correct choice to complete each sentence. (各3点)

1. The government decided to (　　) the outdated law that had been in place for decades.

① abolish　　② create　　③ design　　④ make

2. Careful (　　) made him change his mind.

① application　　② celebration　　③ reconsideration　　④ rejection

3. The company had to close down its (　　) division due to financial losses.

① innovative　　② productive　　③ profitable　　④ unprofitable

4. You can't enter the building (　　) you have a security badge.

① although　　② unless　　③ until　　④ while

5. She decided to (　　) her application for the job after receiving a better offer from another company.

① accept　　② expect　　③ submit　　④ withdraw

6. Vitamins and minerals are (　　) for a healthy diet.

① essential　　② expendable　　③ optional　　④ unnecessary

✐ **Production (Write)**　自分の考えを書いて伝えよう【思考力・判断力・表現力】

Write your answer to the following question. (10点)

Do you have any requests for your local authority?

アドバイス　local authority「自治体」

[A]

Vincent van Gogh (1853-90) //

　Vincent van Gogh was a Dutch painter / who went to live / in southern France / and who helped develop the style / of Post-Impressionism. // His paintings / **typically** use bright colors / and have thick lines of paint / in **circular** patterns, / and the most famous ones include Sunflowers and **Irises**. // Although he wasn't famous / during his **lifetime**, / today / he is considered / one of the greatest / and most influential artists / of his time. // His paintings are now **extremely valuable** / and are sold / for very high prices. //

[B]

　[…]

　One of the reasons / why I'm now without a **position**, / why I've been without a position / for years, / is quite simply because I have different ideas / from these gentlemen / who give positions / to individuals / who think like them. //

　It's not a simple matter / of appearance, / it's something / more serious / than that, / I **assure** you. //

　[…]

　Well, / that's not quite how it is; / what has changed is / that my life was less difficult / then / and my future less dark, / but as far as my **inner** self, / as far as my way of seeing and thinking are concerned, / they haven't changed. // But if / in fact / there were a change, / it's that now I think / and I believe / and I love / more seriously / what then, / too, / I already thought, / I believed and I loved. //

　[…]

　Letter to Theo van Gogh. // June 1880 // (223 words)

◀) 音読しよう

Practice 1　スラッシュ位置で文を区切って読んでみよう □

Practice 2　英語の強弱のリズムに注意して読んでみよう □

TRY!　　　2分10秒以内に本文全体を音読しよう □

スピーキング・トレーナー

📖 **Reading**　本文の内容を読んで理解しよう【知識・技能】【思考力・判断力・表現力】　共通テスト

Make the correct choice to complete each sentence or answer each question. (各6点)

1.　What is the current perception of Vincent van Gogh in the art world? ☐

　　① He is not considered influential in the art world.

　　② He is regarded as one of the greatest and most influential artists of his time.

③ He was a famous artist during his lifetime.

④ His paintings are not highly valued or sold for high prices today.

2. Van Gogh believed that he could not succeed [　　　].

　① because he had different ideas than what was expected of him

　② because his appearance does not meet the standards

　③ because his inner self and way of seeing and thinking have changed significantly

　④ because his life had become more difficult, leading to a darker future

🔍 **Vocabulary**　重要表現について理解しよう【知識】　　英検 ® GTEC®

Make the correct choice to complete each sentence. (各4点)

1. (　　　　), students enjoy a break from school during the summer months.

　① Deliberately　　② Occasionally　　③ Rapidly　　④ Typically

2. The figure is perfectly (　　　) because it was drawn using a compass.

　① circular　　② rectangular　　③ spherical　　④ valuable

3. His performance in the game was (　　　) impressive!

　① extremely　　② gradually　　③ moderately　　④ slightly

4. The manager wanted to (　　　) customers that their satisfaction was a top priority.

　① appreciate　　② assure　　③ estimate　　④ ignore

5. The (　　　) workings of the company are not always visible to the public.

　① external　　② inner　　③ outer　　④ superficial

✐ **Production (Write)**　自分の考えを書いて伝えよう【思考力・判断力・表現力】

Write your answer to the following question. (8点)

　Have you ever been moved by a painting?

　アドバイス　そのときのことを描写してみよう。

13

You are studying / about sea turtles. //　You found two articles / about them. //

Sea Turtle //

　Sea turtles are one of the oldest kinds of animals. // They have been around / for over 100 million years. // They are generally larger / than land turtles. // Some sea turtles are huge. // They weigh / up to 400 **pounds** / (180 kilograms). // Large sea turtles can swim / up to 5.8 miles / (9.3 kilometers) / per hour. // Sea turtles live / in the deep ocean / most of the year. // For this reason, / scientists do not know / much about their behavior. // But they know / that sea turtles move around / a lot / to find food. // Sea turtles can travel / hundreds or thousands of miles / every year. // Some kinds of sea turtles eat / only plants. // Others eat plants, / shellfish, / or other sea animals. //

Sea Turtle Conservation Program //

　The number of sea turtles has been decreasing / worldwide / due to human influences. // Chemicals and pollution of the water / from **trash** / cause health problems / for sea turtles. // **Ingestion** of fishing nets, / lines and **hooks** are other dangers. // Sea turtles caught in fishing nets / cannot reach the surface / to breathe. // **Overdeveloped coastal** areas / have destroyed the area / of their natural nesting environment / and increased **lighting misguides** baby turtles / and nesting mothers. // Especially / during the **mating**, / nesting, / and **hatching** seasons, / people need / to be careful / as sea turtles can be mostly found at / or just below the surface / in coastal waters. // Only 0.1 percent of baby turtles / that enter the ocean will survive / and become adults. // This is due to all the natural / and human-made dangers / they face. // For these reasons, / all sea turtle species should be protected. // (256 words)

🔊 **音読しよう**　　　　　　　　　　　　　　　　　　スピーキング・トレーナー
Practice 1　スラッシュ位置で文を区切って読んでみよう □
Practice 2　英語の強弱のリズムに注意して読んでみよう □
TRY!　　　　2分30秒以内に本文全体を音読しよう □

📖 Reading　本文の内容を読んで理解しよう【知識・技能】【思考力・判断力・表現力】　　共通テスト

Make the correct choice to answer each question. (各6点)

1. What is the primary reason for the decreasing number of sea turtles worldwide?

① Human influences, including pollution and coastal development [　　]

② Lack of suitable nesting sites

③ Natural predators

④ Overpopulation of sea turtles

2. Which of the following is true about sea turtles? [　　]

① Sea turtles are often found in the deeper layers of the ocean, but can be found near the surface at certain periods.

② Sea turtles travel very long distances in search of waters with unpolluted water quality.

③ The behavior of sea turtles is still poorly understood, and it remains unclear why their numbers are declining.

④ The global decline in the number of plants that sea turtles eat has led to a series of cases of sea turtles eating fishing lines and other items.

🔍 Vocabulary　重要表現について理解しよう【知識】　　英検® GTEC®

Make the correct choice to complete each sentence. (各4点)

1. Please make sure to dispose of your (　　　　) in the designated bins.
　　① jewelry　　　　② secret　　　　③ trash　　　　④ treasure

2. The plan to (　　　) the area raised concerns about environmental impact.
　　① green　　　　② overdevelop　　　　③ preserve　　　　④ reduce

3. (　　　　) areas are vulnerable to sea-level rise due to climate change.
　　① Coastal　　　　② Desert　　　　③ Inland　　　　④ Mountainous

4. Penguins often (　　　) for life and share responsibility for raising chicks.
　　① compete　　　　② mate　　　　③ migrate　　　　④ nest

5. The baby turtles will (　　　　) from their eggs in about two months.
　　① hatch　　　　② remove　　　　③ swim　　　　④ vanish

✐ Production (Write)　自分の考えを書いて伝えよう【思考力・判断力・表現力】

Write your answer to the following question. (8点)

Write one thing you can do to protect sea turtles.

アドバイス　どうしてそれがウミガメの保護につながるのかも説明しよう。

Japan is now **constructing** / a **maglev** train system / between Tokyo and Nagoya. // This train system is based / on advanced **bullet** train technology / developed in Japan. //

① The Shinkansen, / Japan's bullet trains, / **zoomed** onto the **railway** scene / on October 1, 1964. // It was just nine days / before the Tokyo Olympic Games began. // The Hikari, / then the fastest train, / **shrank** travel time / between Tokyo and Osaka / to less than half / of what it was **previously**. // Now the **network** has **expanded** / to over 3,000 kilometers of lines. //

② The Shinkansen was originally constructed / to reinforce the transportation **capacity** / of the Tokaido Line of Japanese National Railways, / in order to meet the needs / of **rapid** economic growth. // Since then, / the railway network / has played an important role / in the development of Japan. //

③ The Japanese bullet train was the first high-speed railway system / in the world. // It was also a symbol / of Japan's **recovery** / from the **devastation** / of World War II. // Even today, / it remains one of the fastest train networks / in the world / and shows the highly-developed train technology / of Japan. // The Shinkansen has **demonstrated** / the importance and advantages / of high-speed railways. // Its success has had a great influence / on other railways / in the world. // Many countries are now constructing / and expanding high-speed railway networks. // (167 words)

🔊 **音読しよう**　　　　　　　　　　　　　　　　　　　スピーキング・トレーナー

Practice 1　スラッシュ位置で文を区切って読んでみよう ☐
Practice 2　英語の強弱のリズムに注意して読んでみよう ☐
TRY!　　　　1分40秒以内に本文全体を音読しよう ☐

📖 **Reading**　本文の内容を読んで理解しよう【知識・技能】【思考力・判断力・表現力】　　　共通テスト

Make the correct choice to complete each sentence or answer each question. (各4点)

1. The Shinkansen ☐.

　① had a network that expanded over 3,000 kilometers of lines in 1964

　② made its first appearance in 1964

　③ shrank travel time between Tokyo and Okayama to less than half of what it was previously in 1964

　④ started running after the Tokyo Olympic Games began

2. How has the railway network contributed to the development of Japan? ☐

　① By improving environmental sustainability.

　② By meeting the needs of rapid economic growth.

　③ By providing faster transportation for tourists.

　④ By reducing traffic congestion on the roads.

◀ 英語の強弱のリズムを理解して音読することができる。	📖 高速鉄道の発達に関する英文を読んで，概要や要点を捉えることができる。
🔍 文脈を理解して適切な語句を用いて英文を完成することができる。	🎧 平易な英語で話される短い英文を聞いて必要な情報を聞き取ることができる。
🗨 新幹線について情報を伝えることができる。	💬 旅行の経験について説明することができる。

Goals

3. The Japanese bullet train was the symbol of ☐.

① Japan's commitment to environmental sustainability

② Japan's desire to attract more tourists

③ Japan's economic boom

④ Japan's recovery from World War II

🔍 Vocabulary & Grammar 重要表現や文法事項について理解しよう【知識】 英検® GTEC®

Make the correct choice to complete each sentence. (各2点)

1. Our government has decided to (   ) a new dam.
   ① compose   ② concern   ③ construct   ④ contact

2. The company is planning to (   ) the office space in Tokyo branch.
   ① exaggerate   ② expand   ③ evacuate   ④ exit

3. One of this camera's problems is the battery (   ).
   ① capacity   ② capital   ③ cause   ④ consistency

4. The president announced his financial statement and (   ) plan at a meeting.
   ① recovery   ② reduction   ③ refusal   ④ regret

5. My great-grandmother experienced the (   ) of the atomic bomb in Hiroshima.
   ① determination   ② destroy   ③ devastation   ④ device

🎧 Listening 英文を聞いて理解しよう【知識・技能】【思考力・判断力・表現力】 共通テスト CD 1

Listen to the English and make the best choice to match the content. (4点)

① The speaker hasn't taken the Shinkansen since he was seventeen.

② The speaker took the Shinkansen seventeen years ago.

③ The speaker took the Shinkansen when he was twenty-one.

💬 Interaction 英文を聞いて会話を続けよう【知識・技能】【思考力・判断力・表現力】 スピーキング・トレーナー CD 2

Listen to the English and respond to the last remark. (7点)

［メモ   ］

アドバイス Yes か No を答えるだけではなく，補足情報を加えて会話を続けよう。

💬 Production (Speak) 自分の考えを話して伝えよう【思考力・判断力・表現力】 スピーキング・トレーナー

Speak out your answer to the following question. (7点)

Have you ever traveled by Shinkansen? How was it?

アドバイス 旅行中のできごとなどを描写して伝えよう。

④ The Tokaido Shinkansen is one of the world's busiest high-speed lines. // In 2017, / it carried / as many as 465,600 **passengers** / on 368 trains / per day / at time **intervals** of just three to six minutes. // In short, / the Japanese bullet train is an **effective** means / of high-speed and high-**frequency mass** transportation. //

⑤ Japan has **geological** conditions / **unsuitable** for bullet trains. // **Mountainous terrain** / with only small plain areas / has made it difficult / to extend the tracks / for high-speed railways. // Various other **factors**, / such as **frequent** earthquakes, / many volcanic mountains, / typhoons in summer and autumn, / and heavy snows in winter / have threatened the safe and **accurate operation** / of the trains. //

⑥ With all these **disadvantages**, / the Shinkansen **deserves** great praise / for having the highest level / of safety and efficiency / in the world. // The service has continued / to work well over the decades. // According to Central Japan Railway, / the average delay from **schedule** / per train / is an amazingly low 36 seconds. // It has maintained a record / of no passenger **fatalities** / resulting from train accidents / since its debut. // The Shinkansen stands / as a global symbol / of Japanese technological innovation / that has been studied / by many other countries. // (190 words)

🔊 **音読しよう**　　　　　　　　　　　　　　　　　　スピーキング・トレーナー

Practice 1　スラッシュ位置で文を区切って読んでみよう □
Practice 2　英語の強弱のリズムに注意して読んでみよう □
TRY!　　　1分50秒以内に本文全体を音読しよう □

📖 **Reading**　　本文の内容を読んで理解しよう【知識・技能】【思考力・判断力・表現力】　　共通テスト

Make the correct choice to complete each sentence or answer each question. (各4点)

1. The Tokaido Shinkansen is ☐ .

　① one of the busiest high-speed lines in the world

　② the fastest train in the world

　③ the longest high-speed line in the world

　④ the oldest high-speed line in the world

2. What makes it difficult to extend the tracks for high-speed railways in Japan? ☐

　① Frequent earthquakes

　② Heavy snows in winter

　③ Mountainous terrain with only small plain areas

　④ Typhoons in summer and autumn

◀) 英語の強弱のリズムを理解して音読することができる。	📖 新幹線の特色に関する英文を読んで，概要や要点を捉えることができる。
🔍 文脈を理解して適切な語句を用いて英文を完成することができる。	◌ 平易な英語で話される短い英文を聞いて必要な情報を聞き取ることができる。
🔊 時刻表について考えを表現することができる。	✎ 日本の技術革新について考えを表現することができる。

Goals

3. From paragraph 6, you can see that the Japanese bullet trains ☐ .

① are very safe   ② run very frequently

③ should be extended   ④ have overcome many accidents

🔍 Vocabulary & Grammar   重要表現や文法事項について理解しよう【知識】   英検® GTEC®

Make the correct choice to complete each sentence. (各2点)

1. Although Tom's girlfriend got angry with him, he didn't say sorry to her. (   ), I think he made a big mistake.

① In addition   ② In short   ③ Instead   ④ In time

2. These shoes are (   ) for this dress so I want to change them before the ceremony.

① unknown   ② unreal   ③ unsuitable   ④ useful

3. He is a (   ) who ordered the vegetarian meal online in advance.

① permission   ② passage   ③ passenger   ④ pattern

4. The (   ) survey in this mountain will have been completed by the end of next year.

① geological   ② legendary   ③ likely   ④ memorial

5. Finally, our group got (   ) figures after many tests.

① accurate   ② advanced   ③ automatical   ④ clean

🎧 Listening   英文を聞いて理解しよう【知識・技能】【思考力・判断力・表現力】   共通テスト   CD 3

Listen to the English and make the best choice to match the content. (4点)

① All of the trains have been canceled until noon.

② Not all of the trains will stop running tomorrow.

③ The railway company plans to cancel onboard announcements tomorrow morning.

💬 Interaction   英文を聞いて会話を続けよう【知識・技能】【思考力・判断力・表現力】   スピーキング・トレーナー   CD 4

Listen to the English and respond to the last remark. (7点)

[メモ   ]

アドバイス   知っているかどうかだけでなく，利用したことがあるかなどを付け加えよう。

✎ Production (Write)   自分の考えを書いて伝えよう【思考力・判断力・表現力】

Write your answer to the following question. (7点)

Do you know any other Japanese innovations?

アドバイス   ハイブリッド車や，インスタントラーメン，温水洗浄便座，青色LEDなどが例として挙げられる。それが innovation であると思う理由を書いて伝えよう。

⑦ In Japan, / **superconducting** maglev trains, / or **linear** motor cars, / are expected / to make their debut / in the near future. // The system uses a driving force / from power / generated by **electromagnets**. // The action of the **magnets** / holds the train up / and **ensures** the existence of a **gap** / between the **rails** and the train. // Not touching the rails, // the train avoids any loss of speed / caused by **friction** / between the rails and the wheels. //

⑧ This system will allow the train / to run much faster / and to cause far less noise / than the **current** bullet train. // The maglev train / which is now under **construction** / will be the fastest train / in the world, / with a speed of about 500 k.p.h. // It will enable people / to travel / between Tokyo and Nagoya / in about 40 minutes. //

⑨ High-speed railways are entering a new stage. // Trains are more environmentally friendly / than airplanes / and gasoline cars / in that they use electricity / as a source of power. // They use less energy / and produce less CO_2. // More and more people are now becoming aware / of the need / for environmental protection / and energy conservation. // The day will soon arrive / when high-speed railways will play a leading role / in transportation / **throughout** the world. // (157 words)

◀)) 音読しよう   スピーキング・トレーナー
Practice 1   スラッシュ位置で文を区切って読んでみよう □
Practice 2   英語の強弱のリズムに注意して読んでみよう □
TRY!   1分30秒以内に本文全体を音読しよう □

📖 Reading   本文の内容を読んで理解しよう【知識・技能】【思考力・判断力・表現力】   共通テスト

Make the correct choice to complete each sentence or answer each question. (各4点)

1. [　　] is used to drive maglev trains or linear motor cars.
   ① Power generated by electromagnets
   ② Power generated by friction between magnets and rails
   ③ Power generated by natural gas in the magnets
   ④ Power generated by some chemical reactions

2. Which of the following is true about the maglev train? [　　]
   ① It will be the fastest train in the world.
   ② It will be the noisiest train in Japan.
   ③ It will cause more friction between the rails and the wheels than the Shinkansen.
   ④ It will enable people to travel between Tokyo and Osaka in about 40 minutes.

英語の強弱のリズムを理解して音読することができる。	リニア新幹線に関する英文を読んで，概要や要点を捉えることができる。
文脈を理解して適切な語句を用いて英文を完成することができる。	平易な英語で話される短い英文を聞いて必要な情報を聞き取ることができる。

Goals

リニア新幹線について考えを伝えることができる。

3. High-speed railways [＿＿＿].

① will be less popular in the world

② will meet the demand for environmental protection

③ will replace the role of airplanes

④ will use less energy than gasoline cars but produce more CO_2

🔍 Vocabulary & Grammar　重要表現や文法事項について理解しよう【知識】　英検® GTEC®

Make the correct choice to complete each sentence. (各2点)

1. (　　　) enough time, I didn't have breakfast.

　① Having had　　② Not had　　③ Never had　　④ Not having

2. A new shopping mall is (　　　) construction near the station.

　① during　　② in　　③ over　　④ under

3. There is a big (　　　) between the two countries about food security issue.

　① gap　　② management　　③ unreality　　④ victory

4. Please write down your (　　　) address here.

　① potential　　② incorrect　　③ current　　④ known

5. The weather is mild in this country. It is warm (　　　) the year.

　① across　　② beyond　　③ throughout　　④ except

🎧 Listening　英文を聞いて理解しよう【知識・技能】【思考力・判断力・表現力】　共通テスト CD 5

Listen to the English and make the best choice to match the content. (4点)

　① It takes less than two hours to travel from the speaker's home to Tokyo currently.

　② Probably the speaker lives very far from Tokyo.

　③ The speaker can see the maglev train traveling extremely fast.

💬 Interaction　英文を聞いて会話を続けよう【知識・技能】【思考力・判断力・表現力】　スピーキング・トレーナー CD 6

Listen to the English and respond to the last remark. (7点)

［メモ　　　　　　　　　　　　　　　　　　　　　　　　　　　　　　　　　　　]

アドバイス　相手の気持ちに対してコメントをしてあげよう。

✏️ Production (Write)　自分の考えを書いて伝えよう【思考力・判断力・表現力】

Write your answer to the following question. (7点)

　Do you think maglev trains will be more convenient than other transportation?

アドバイス　自分が実生活でリニア新幹線を使うときのことを想像してみよう。

After learning / about the development of high-speed railways, / a student wrote a short **essay** / about one of his memories / of railway travel / in an English class. //

　When I was younger, / my father often took my family / on several-day trips. // I remember visiting Mt. Aso, / Himeji Castle, / the Japan **Alps**, / and other places. // All these trips were great fun, / but there was one thing / I didn't like so much. // Many times, / though not always, / we made a trip / by car. // My father drove his car / all the way / during the trip, / because he really likes driving. // Traveling by car / was convenient and **inexpensive** / for my family, / to be sure, / but going along an **expressway** / for many hours / made me bored and sleepy. //

　I remember making a family trip / to Noto **Peninsula** / by train / when I was twelve years old. // We took a limited express train / to Kanazawa, / where we changed to a local train / that ran much slower / and stopped at every station. // It took us / a long time / to reach the station / where we got off, / but I had a very good time / on the train. // Looking out of the window of the train, / I enjoyed the scenery / of mountains, sea, **coastline** and local towns / that we couldn't have seen / from a car on an expressway. //

　I think slower trains enable us / to enjoy travel / in a more relaxed way. // Faster trains, / such as the Shinkansen, / are very convenient / for business trips and commuting long distances, / but in my free time / I would like to travel by slower trains / when possible. // (184 words)

🔊 **音読しよう**　　　　　　　　　　　　　　　　　　　　　スピーキング・トレーナー

Practice 1　スラッシュ位置で文を区切って読んでみよう ☐
Practice 2　英語の強弱のリズムに注意して読んでみよう ☐
TRY!　　　　１分50秒以内に本文全体を音読しよう ☐

📖 **Reading**　本文の内容を読んで理解しよう【知識・技能】【思考力・判断力・表現力】　　共通テスト

Make the correct choice to complete each sentence or answer each question. (各4点)

1. When the student was younger, he felt that ☐ .

　① traveling by car to the Japan Alps was impressive

　② traveling by car was boring although it was inexpensive

　③ traveling by car was exciting because the views from the window were beautiful

　④ traveling by car was the best means of transportation

2. How did the student feel about their family trip to Noto Peninsula by train? ☐

　① He enjoyed the scenery and relaxed atmosphere.

　② He felt it was inconvenient and uncomfortable.

　③ He found it boring and slow.

　④ He thought it was too expensive.

3. Which of the following is **not** correct about the student's essay? ☐

① He had a good memory about the trip to Noto Peninsula by train.

② He thinks that the Shinkansen is very convenient for business trips.

③ His family took one-day trips every year.

④ His father really likes driving.

🔍 **Vocabulary & Grammar**　重要表現や文法事項について理解しよう【知識】　英検® GTEC®

Make the correct choice to complete each sentence. (各2点)

1. (　　　) busy, Nancy relaxed at home and enjoyed playing video games.
　① Never had been　② Never have been　③ Not been　④ Not being

2. Mark ran (　　　) to school because he got up late.
　① all the way　② no way　③ out of the way　④ under way

3. She is right, (　　　), but I can't agree with her.
　① be sure to　② to be sure　③ to not be sure　④ making sure

4. I have to write (　　　) on the book I read during summer vacation.
　① a statement　② a suggestion　③ an album　④ an essay

5. Look at this picture! I took a trip to Izu (　　　) last weekend.
　① Lake　② Peninsula　③ Pond　④ River

6. If you go to the zoo, (　　　) at the next station.
　① get along with　② get off　③ get out of　④ get rid of

7. You can get an (　　　) used car online. Please check our website soon!
　① impossible　② inexpensive　③ influential　④ instant

8. This (　　　) is famous for its beautiful white sand.
　① coastline　② hill　③ seal　④ wave

🎧 **Listening**　英文を聞いて理解しよう【知識・技能】【思考力・判断力・表現力】　共通テスト CD 7

Listen to the English and make the best choice to match the content. (各4点)

1. Where did the speaker and their friends stop to buy lunch on their way to Karuizawa?
　① At Karuizawa.　② At Yokokawa.　③ At Tokyo.　④ At Nagano.

2. How many times did the speaker went to summer camp by local train?
　① Only once.　② Twice.　③ Three times.　④ Four times.

3. Why did the speaker feel sorry?

① Because he thought he could go to the camp by Shinkansen.

② Because he thought he might forget the taste of the ekiben box lunch.

③ Because he thought he would never experience the same journey again.

④ Because he thought the Shinkansen wouldn't stop at Yokokawa for ten minutes.

Many of us take safe drinking water for **granted**, / even though more than 600 million people / worldwide / must depend on / unclean water / every day. //

① In many parts of Africa / and some **Southeast** Asian countries, / there is no tap water. // In many cases, / women and children have to use / river water / for their everyday needs. // It takes them hours / to carry it home. // They may be attacked / by dangerous wild animals / on their way. // The task of carrying water / every day / is so tough / that many children cannot go to school. //

② What is worse, / the water people depend on / is often **muddy** or unclean. // Even after they safely return home, / the polluted water sometimes causes **fatal** diseases / like **cholera**. // Some families have their own wells, / but / unless the wells are deep enough, / the water in them / may be **contaminated**. //

③ The need for water / can **trigger conflicts** / between groups of people. // In Kenya, / two **tribes** were on the **verge** of fighting / each other / over the water / from a river. // A farming tribe / living in a village **upstream** / made a dam / for their crops, / and the **herding** tribe / living **downstream** / got so angry / that they armed themselves / in preparation / for **retaking** the water. // Fortunately, / the police **intervened** / in the **dispute**, / and fighting was **narrowly** avoided. // (188 words)

🔊 **音読しよう**　　　　　　　　　　　　　　　　　　　スピーキング・トレーナー
Practice 1　スラッシュ位置で文を区切って読んでみよう □
Practice 2　英語の強弱のリズムに注意して読んでみよう □
TRY!　　　　１分50秒以内に本文全体を音読しよう □

📖 **Reading**　本文の内容を読んで理解しよう【知識・技能】【思考力・判断力・表現力】　　共通テスト

Make the correct choice to complete each sentence or answer each question. (各 4 点)

1. In many parts of Africa and some Southeast Asian countries with no tap water, _____.
   ① dangerous animals attack people for water
   ② some children cannot attend school because they are too busy collecting water
   ③ many old people have to carry water from river
   ④ women and children have to go to school to get bottled water for their family

2. Which of the following is true about people in areas without tap water? _____
   ① They have switched from river water to well water as technology has improved.
   ② Some families own wells but they sometimes lead to conflict.
   ③ The polluted water could kill people who drink it.
   ④ The wells they have are usually deep enough to take clean water.

◀)) 英語の強弱のリズムを理解して音読することができる。
🔎 文脈を理解して適切な語句を用いて英文を完成することができる。
🔎 水について簡単な語句を用いて考えを表現することができる。
📖 世界の水問題に関する英文を読んで，概要や要点を捉えることができる。
🎧 平易な英語で話される短い英文を聞いて必要な情報を聞き取ることができる。
💬 飲み水について簡単な語句を用いて考えを表現することができる。

Goals

3. In Kenya, [   ].

① a farming tribe and the herding tribe fought each other over water

② the intervention of the police barely stopped the struggle between two tribes

③ there are many causes of conflict between the village people and the government

④ two tribes were on the verge of fighting over more land

🔎 Vocabulary & Grammar   重要表現や文法事項について理解しよう【知識】   英検® GTEC®

Make the correct choice to complete each sentence. (各2点)

1. This small pond used to be (   ) by bacteria. But thanks to the latest technology, it has clean water now.

① contained   ② contaminated   ③ continued   ④ convinced

2. Ted fell down the stairs of the station yesterday and (   ), lost his wallet.

① what happened   ② what is better   ③ what is called   ④ what is worse

3. Most people (   ) good health for granted until they get sick.

① become   ② carry   ③ get   ④ take

4. The little girl appeared to be (   ) tears when she found herself all alone.

① at the site of   ② by the name of   ③ in the nick of   ④ on the verge of

5. This road will (   ) you to the station.

① confuse   ② divert   ③ intervene   ④ lead

🎧 Listening   英文を聞いて理解しよう【知識・技能】【思考力・判断力・表現力】   共通テスト CD 8

Listen to the English and make the best choice to match the content. (4点)

① The speaker encourages us not to drink the water from the well.

② The speaker regrets cooking with the water from the well.

③ The speaker says we shouldn't use river water for cooking and drinking.

💬 Interaction   英文を聞いて会話を続けよう【知識・技能】【思考力・判断力・表現力】   スピーキング・トレーナー CD 9

Listen to the English and respond to the last remark. (7点)

[メモ   ]

アドバイス 普段の生活で水を使う場面を考えよう。また，水がない場合の代替方法についても想像しよう。

💬 Production (Speak)   自分の考えを話して伝えよう【思考力・判断力・表現力】   スピーキング・トレーナー

Speak out your answer to the following question. (7点)

Do you usually drink tap water or bottled water?

アドバイス どうしてその選択をしているのか理由を述べよう。

----

④ Atsushi Ono, / who used to work / as a construction site **supervisor**, / found an article / published by an NGO. // It was about digging wells / for clean water / in **Zambia** / with the traditional Japanese method / called *Kazusabori*. // This article **reminded** him / of his grandfather, / who was a well-**driller**, / and he became interested / in the project. //

⑤ *Kazusabori* was developed / in the Kazusa area / in Chiba Prefecture. // Drillers can dig / into the ground / as deep as several hundred meters / until fresh **underground** water comes out. // This method only requires human power / and building materials / that are available locally. // Although its use declined / in Japan / after the machine-drilling system was developed, / this method has been welcomed / in developing countries. //

⑥ Ono applied / to join the project and, / thanks to his experience / in construction, / he was chosen / as a member. // After training / in digging wells / and speaking English, / he went to Meheba, / a town / in the northern part of Zambia, / where there were many refugees / from neighboring countries. // Ono's team began digging, / and when the **depth** of the well reached / about 25 meters, / water came out. // That was the moment / when his first well was successful. // (189 words)

🔊 **音読しよう**　　　　　　　　　　　　　　　　　　　スピーキング・トレーナー
Practice 1　スラッシュ位置で文を区切って読んでみよう☐
Practice 2　英語の強弱のリズムに注意して読んでみよう☐
TRY!　　　　1分50秒以内に本文全体を音読しよう☐

📖 **Reading**　本文の内容を読んで理解しよう【知識・技能】【思考力・判断力・表現力】　　共通テスト

Make the correct choice to complete each sentence or answer each question. (各4点)

1. Which of the following is **not** true about Atsushi Ono? ☐
   ① He had some experiences in digging wells in Japan.
   ② He read the news of an NGO organizing a project in Zambia.
   ③ He worked at construction sites as a supervisor.
   ④ His grandfather knew how to dig wells.

2. *Kazusabori* ☐.
   ① costs more than machine-drilling　② doesn't require any special materials
   ③ needs no human power at all　④ was named after a person who invented it

3. Put the events in the order they occurred. ☐ → ☐ → ☐ → ☐ → ☐

① Ono trained in digging wells and speaking English.

② Ono went to a town in Zambia.

③ Ono worked as a construction site supervisor.

④ Ono's first well-digging project was successful.

⑤ Ono's team started digging a well.

🔍 Vocabulary & Grammar 　重要表現や文法事項について理解しよう【知識】　　英検® GTEC®

Make the correct choice to complete each sentence. （各2点）

1. The song always (　　　) me of the day I met him for the first time.

   ① recalls　　　② recognizes　　　③ remembers　　　④ reminds

2. How do researchers measure the (　　　) of the ocean?

   ① deep　　　② depth　　　③ distance　　　④ length

3. Look! Smoke is (　　　) out of the kitchen!

   ① coming　　　② getting　　　③ running　　　④ taking

4. Amy took over the responsibility from the (　　　).

   ① superstition　　　② supervisor　　　③ surface　　　④ survivor

5. The door to the (　　　) tunnel was hidden behind the wall.

   ① unauthorized　　　② uncomfortable　　　③ underground　　　④ unfortunate

🎧 Listening 　英文を聞いて理解しよう【知識・技能】【思考力・判断力・表現力】　共通テスト CD 10

Listen to the English and make the best choice to match the content. （4点）

① The speaker explains how deep he will dig the well.

② The speaker teaches us very well how to get water from the ground.

③ The speaker wants to know about digging a well.

💬 Interaction 　英文を聞いて会話を続けよう【知識・技能】【思考力・判断力・表現力】　スピーキング・トレーナー CD 11

Listen to the English and respond to the last remark. （7点）

［メモ　　］

アドバイス　最初に質問をしているのはあなたです。知らない場合も，説明を求めて会話を続けよう。

✏️ Production（Write）　自分の考えを書いて伝えよう【思考力・判断力・表現力】

Write your answer to the following question. （7点）

You met a student who wants to contribute to improving the quality of life in developing countries. What do you think he should do?

アドバイス　対面した相手にアドバイスをしている場面ではないことに注意。

----

7 During his work, / Ono trained the local people / so that they could continue / to dig wells / on their own. // He taught them / to replace the materials / used in traditional *Kazusabori* / with more **suitable** ones / for Africa. // He also changed some **technical** Japanese terms / into plain English words. // There is a saying / he **cherishes**: / "If your friends are hungry, / do not give them / fish, / but teach them / how to catch / them." // He thinks / that teaching well-digging techniques / to local people / is better / than simply making wells / for them. //

8 Ono later established an NPO, / the International Water Project (IWP). // Although there have been many hardships / in its operation, / it has completed / more than 100 wells / so far. // Besides digging wells, / the members are teaching children / the importance of planting and growing trees / for the future. //

9 A supply of clean water ensures improved health, / good education, / and work opportunities. // **Universal** and **equitable access** / to safe and **affordable** drinking water / is one of the SDG targets / which we need to achieve / by 2030. // The traditional Japanese *Kazusabori* method / is playing an important role / in achieving this target. // (183 words)

🔊 **音読しよう**　　　　　　　　　　　　　　　　　　　スピーキング・トレーナー
Practice 1　スラッシュ位置で文を区切って読んでみよう ☐
Practice 2　英語の強弱のリズムに注意して読んでみよう ☐
TRY!　　　　１分50秒以内に本文全体を音読しよう ☐

📖 **Reading**　本文の内容を読んで理解しよう【知識・技能】【思考力・判断力・表現力】　　共通テスト

Make the correct choice to complete each sentence or answer each question. (各 4 点)

1. "If your friends are hungry, do not give them fish, but teach them how to catch them." What does this saying imply? ☐
   ① It implies hungry friends usually prefer fish to bread.
   ② It implies hungry people need to know how to cook before catching fish.
   ③ It implies it is more beneficial to teach a person how to do something than to do that something for them.
   ④ It implies you shouldn't spoil your friend who doesn't learn or work.

2. What does the IWP do besides digging wells? ☐
   ① It constructs schools for children.
   ② It negotiates local governments to make a budget for wells.
   ③ It publishes a book to spread the *Kazusabori* method.
   ④ It teaches children the importance of planting and growing trees.

3. According to paragraph 9, a supply of clean water ☐.

① brings healthy and cultural lives to people

② ensures luxury to local people

③ makes one of the SDGs targets withdrawn

④ makes people skilled with well-drilling

🔍 **Vocabulary & Grammar**　重要表現や文法事項について理解しよう【知識】　英検® GTEC®

Make the correct choice to complete each sentence. (各2点)

1. The instructions say this toy is (　　　) for children over 5 years old.

　① accurate　　　② attractive　　　③ proficient　　　④ suitable

2. The teacher ensured that the distribution of grades was (　　　).

　① accessible　　② equitable　　　③ humble　　　④ random

3. (　　　) both your idea and your friends' ideas.

　① Allow　　　② Cherish　　　③ Expect　　　④ Recall

4. A powerful storm (　　　) more than 1,000 flights yesterday.

　① canceled　　② hit　　　③ made　　　④ was caused

5. The new shop provides quality goods at (　　　) prices.

　① affordable　　② cheap　　　③ excess　　　④ valuable

🎧 **Listening**　英文を聞いて理解しよう【知識・技能】【思考力・判断力・表現力】　共通テスト CD 12

Listen to the English and make the best choice to match the content. (4点)

① The NPO couldn't achieve its goal of planting trees.

② The NPO has planted two hundred more trees than its original plan.

③ Currently, the NPO has planted two hundred trees.

🗨 **Interaction**　英文を聞いて会話を続けよう【知識・技能】【思考力・判断力・表現力】　スピーキング・トレーナー CD 13

Listen to the English and respond to the last remark. (7点)

［メ モ　　　　　　　　　　　　　　　　　　　　　　　　　　　　　　　　　　］

アドバイス　見たことがある場合，見たことがない場合でも何か情報を付け加える。

✎ **Production (Write)**　自分の考えを書いて伝えよう【思考力・判断力・表現力】

Write your answer to the following question. (7点)

Choose one of the following three goals of SDG targets that you want to work on. Explain why you chose it.

| 2. Zero Hunger　　4. Quality Education　　7. Affordable and Clean Energy |

アドバイス　理由が論理的になるように注意しよう。

You are looking / at a **crowdfunding** website / and discussing / which group you will donate to. //

Water for **Cambodia** //

Reward: / Local farm products / like **raw** sugar //

Be the first to donate / $0 of $5,000 //

Cambodia is a nation / rich in water. // The water in many areas / is clean / and **drinkable**. // Nevertheless, / the ground / in some areas of Cambodia / contains chemicals / **poisonous** to humans. // In such areas, / underground water needs to be **filtered** / with special kinds of plastic **fiber**. // We have been working / for decades / with a Japanese company / which has technology / for filtering water / and have been assisting farmers / in Cambodia. //

Water for **Myanmar** //

Reward: / A piece of **handicraft** //

Last donation: / 7h ago / $3,700 of $7,500 //

Sea water is available / to many people / in areas / along sea **coasts**, / especially in the refugee camps / along the coasts of Myanmar / and **Bangladesh**. // When sea water is filtered / with a special fiber, / it becomes fresh water. // Unfortunately, / it often costs / more than 1 US dollar / to make 1 **cubic** meter of fresh water. // With 3 US dollars / a day, / we can provide fresh water / to save the lives / of more than 2 refugees. // Your pocket money will save lives! //

Assistance for India //

Reward: / A package of Indian tea / (for a donation of 20 US dollars / or more) //

Last donation: / 15m ago / $5,900 of $6,000 //

When it comes to filtering, / it costs less / to turn waste water into clean water / than it does / to turn sea water into fresh water. // The processed water can be used / for farming and toilets, / and it also reduces / the large amount of waste water / **flowing** into rivers. // In India, / where waste from toilets is a serious issue, / this project will solve / not only water shortages, / but also **sewage** problems. // We appreciate your help / in improving public **hygiene** / in India.

The **Ugandan** Well Foundation //

Reward: / Your name will be **carved** / into a well //

Last donation: / 7h ago / $15,000 of $10,000 //

The Ugandan Well Foundation, / together with local partners, / provides access / to clean water. // Unfortunately, / we lack money / and cannot purchase enough machines and materials / to drill wells. // Some of the existing wells are old / and need repairing, / but the local people don't know / how to fix them. // We are waiting for your donation. // It costs $2,000 / to build a new well, / and $500 / to fix an old one. // (373 words)

◀) 英語の強弱のリズムを理解して音読することができる。

📖 クラウドファンディングサイトに関する英文を読んで，概要や要点を捉えることができる。

🔍 文脈を理解して適切な語句を用いて英文を完成することができる。　　🎧 やや長めの英文を聞いて必要な情報を聞き取ることができる。

◀) **音読しよう**　　　　　　　　　　　　　　　　　　　　　スピーキング・トレーナー

Practice 1　スラッシュ位置で文を区切って読んでみよう □

Practice 2　英語の強弱のリズムに注意して読んでみよう □

TRY!　　　　3分40秒以内に本文全体を音読しよう □

📖 **Reading**　本文の内容を読んで理解しよう【知識・技能】【思考力・判断力・表現力】　　共通テスト

Make the correct choice to complete each sentence or answer each question. (各6点)

1. Which group's project can be a solution to two water-related problems? ☐
   ① Water for Cambodia　　　　　　　② Water for Myanmar
   ③ Assistance for India　　　　　　　④ The Ugandan Well Foundation

2. If you want your name to be recorded as a donor, you should choose ☐ .
   ① Water for Cambodia　　　　　　　② Water for Myanmar
   ③ Assistance for India　　　　　　　④ The Ugandan Well Foundation

---

🔍 **Vocabulary & Grammar**　重要表現や文法事項について理解しよう【知識】　　英検® GTEC®

Make the correct choice to complete each sentence. (各2点)

1. The spectacular views from the summit will be the (　　　　) when climbing a mountain.
   ① recovery　　　　② refund　　　　③ renewal　　　　④ reward

2. The railway was used to transport (　　　) cotton in the 19th century.
   ① law　　　　　② low　　　　　③ raw　　　　　④ row

3. Rick is very good at (　　　　) pumpkins. His jack-o'-lanterns are very popular.
   ① carving　　　② chopping　　　③ completing　　　④ slicing

4. Most of the rivers in Kobe (　　　) from north to south.
   ① fall　　　　　② flow　　　　　③ transfer　　　　④ turn

5. The company rule (　　　　) employees to wear less formal clothes on Fridays.
   ① allows　　　② has　　　　③ lets　　　　④ makes

🎧 **Listening**　英文を聞いて理解しよう【知識・技能】【思考力・判断力・表現力】　　共通テスト　CD 14

Listen to the English and make the best choice to match the content. (各6点)

1. Which is true about the earthquake occurred in Haiti?
   ① It had a magnitude of 7.0.　　　② It occurred in 2016.
   ③ It is called Matthew.　　　　　④ It killed millions of people.

2. When did a huge hurricane hit Haiti?
   ① After the great earthquake.　　② Before the great earthquake.
   ③ In spring.　　　　　　　　　　④ In summer.

3. What can your one dollar donation do?
   ① It can buy nearly 300 water purification tablets.
   ② It can help Haiti people buy bottles of water.
   ③ It can make 5 liters of dirty water clean.
   ④ It can provide 280 Haitians with pure water.

Athletes as Human Rights Leaders

教科書 p.44

What messages can we get / from athletes / in order to make our society / more **sensitive** / to human rights? //

1 "Well, / what was the message / that you got? // That was more the question. // The point is / to make people start talking," / said professional tennis player / Naomi Osaka / when the interviewer asked her / what message she wanted to send / to the spectators. //

2 Born to a **Haitian** father / and a Japanese mother, / Naomi has become / a **prominent** tennis player. // In the 2020 U.S. Open Championships, / she won seven matches / and got her third grand-slam **trophy**. // In each game, / she appeared with a mask / which had the name / of a different African-American / who had been killed / by white **civilians** / or police officers / for no good reason. // Her "message" was **symbolized** / in the names / on the seven masks / she wore. // She said, / "Before I am an athlete, / I am a black woman." //

3 Another Japanese athlete / who shares a **racial background** / similar to Naomi's / is Rui Hachimura, / the NBA star. // He was born in Toyama City / to a Japanese mother and a **Beninese** father, / so he stood out / in his neighborhood / because of his skin color. // "People looked at me / as if to say, / 'You are different.' // I was always trying / to hide from them," / he recalls. // (192 words)

🔊 **音読しよう**　　　　　　　　　　　　　　　スピーキング・トレーナー

Practice 1　スラッシュ位置で文を区切って読んでみよう ☐
Practice 2　イントネーションに注意して読んでみよう ☐
TRY!　　　　2分以内に本文全体を音読しよう ☐

📖 **Reading**　本文の内容を読んで理解しよう【知識・技能】【思考力・判断力・表現力】　　共通テスト

Make the correct choice to complete each sentence or answer each question. (各4点)

1. When the interviewer asked Naomi Osaka what message she wanted to send, she ☐ .

   ① clearly stated what she had in mind

   ② refused to answer the question

   ③ tried to express her message by asking him a question

   ④ wasn't sure what her message was

2. Which of the following is true about Naomi Osaka? ☐

   ① She refused to receive the grand-slam trophy in the 2020 U.S. Open Championships.

   ② She wanted to talk about racial problem with the spectators after the game.

   ③ She was born in Haiti and has become a remarkable tennis player.

   ④ She wore a black mask in each game in order to send people a "message."

◄») イントネーションを理解して音読することができる。	📖 大坂選手と八村選手に関する英文を読んで，概要や要点を捉えることができる。
🔍 文脈を理解して適切な語句を用いて英文を完成することができる。	🎧 平易な英語で話される短い英文を聞いて必要な情報を聞き取ることができる。
📝 日本人選手について簡単な語句を用いて説明することができる。	💬 スポーツで感動した場面を簡単な語句を用いて説明することができる。

Goals

3. Rui Hachimura ☐.

① shares the message with Naomi Osaka

② used to think that people around him were different from him

③ was always trying to hide from people in his neighborhood

④ was born to Beninese parents in Toyama City

🔍 Vocabulary & Grammar　重要表現や文法事項について理解しよう【知識】　英検® GTEC®

Make the correct choice to complete each sentence.（各2点）

1. In ancient Rome, purple (　　　) the emperor.
   ① generalized　　② realized　　③ symbolized　　④ visualized

2. The house with pink wall (　　　) out in the town.
   ① carries　　② figures　　③ hands　　④ stands

3. Wear your sunglasses.　Eyes are (　　　) to ultraviolet rays.
   ① alternative　　② effective　　③ negative　　④ sensitive

4. The symptom appears to be common in all (　　　) and ethnic groups.
   ① national　　② potential　　③ racial　　④ regional

5. The product is temporarily not (　　　) because of a shortage of some materials.
   ① been made　　② being making　　③ being made　　④ making

🎧 Listening　英文を聞いて理解しよう【知識・技能】【思考力・判断力・表現力】　共通テスト CD 15

Listen to the English and make the best choice to match the content.（4点）

① The speaker doesn't understand what the name on the mask means.

② The speaker probably doesn't know Naomi Osaka.

③ The speaker will learn who wore a mask.

💬 Interaction　英文を聞いて会話を続けよう【知識・技能】【思考力・判断力・表現力】　スピーキング・トレーナー CD 16

Listen to the English and respond to the last remark.（7点）

［メモ　　］

　アドバイス　どんな選手なのか，知っている範囲で付け加えよう。

💬 Production（Speak）　自分の考えを話して伝えよう【思考力・判断力・表現力】　スピーキング・トレーナー

Speak out your answer to the following question.（7点）

What's the most impressive sports moment you have seen?

　アドバイス　スポーツを見て感動した場面を発表する。

---

④ Rui was born a natural athlete. // He was very good at all sorts of sports, / and people around him began / to respect him. // He started playing basketball / in junior high school, / and eventually / he became an NBA player. // Rui said, / "I started / to think it's good / to be who I am. // I'm unique. // I'm always proud / of myself." // He supported the movement / against racial **discrimination** / together / with his teammates / by **kneeling** / during the national **anthem** / before games. //

⑤ The world of sports / has had a strong **relationship** / with social issues / for a long time. // However, / while many **biracial** athletes have given great performances / in Japan, / it has been very rare / that these athletes, / let alone other non-biracial Japanese athletes, / have raised their voices / about human rights. // Japanese athletes particularly / "tend to think / it is a **virtue** / to focus only on their own competitions, / not on social issues. // It's a pity," / says Dai Tamesue, / an **Olympian**. //

⑥ It is not only in Japan / that athletics and social issues / have been kept separate. // The International Olympic **Committee** (IOC) / has long tried / to separate itself / from **politics** / in society. // (184 words)

🔊 **音読しよう**

スピーキング・トレーナー

Practice 1　スラッシュ位置で文を区切って読んでみよう ☐
Practice 2　イントネーションに注意して読んでみよう ☐
TRY!　　　 １分50秒以内に本文全体を音読しよう ☐

📖 **Reading**　本文の内容を読んで理解しよう【知識・技能】【思考力・判断力・表現力】　　共通テスト

Make the correct choice to complete each sentence or answer each question. (各4点)

1. Which of the following is true about Rui Hachimura? ☐
   ① He protested against gender discrimination by kneeling.
   ② He has gained confidence and is now proud of himself.
   ③ He started playing basketball in junior high school and later became an MLB player.
   ④ He was good at basketball but not at other sports.

2. According to Dai Tamesue, what is a pity? ☐
   ① Racial discrimination has not been regarded as a serious human right issue in Japan.
   ② Japanese athletes don't concentrate on their performances.
   ③ Japanese athletes seldom speak out on social issues.
   ④ There are few non-biracial athletes who succeed on a global stage.

3. According to paragraph 6, athletics and social issues ☐.

   ① have been closely linked for a long time

   ② have been connected by the International Olympic Committee recently

   ③ have been kept separate only in Japan

   ④ have been separated by the International Olympic Committee for a long time

🔍 **Vocabulary & Grammar**　重要表現や文法事項について理解しよう【知識】　　英検® GTEC®

Make the correct choice to complete each sentence. (各2点)

1. I can't afford a smartphone, (　　　) alone a new car.

   ① have　　　　② leave　　　　③ let　　　　④ make

2. People started to (　　　) their voices in protest.

   ① find　　　　② open　　　　③ raise　　　　④ speak

3. Ted was finally chosen as the chairperson of the (　　　).

   ① commerce　　② commission　　③ committee　　④ communication

4. The bond between them was far beyond a simple patient-doctor (　　　).

   ① association　② connection　　③ hardship　　④ relationship

5. The school taught their students the (　　　) of hard work.

   ① affect　　　② role　　　　③ virtue　　　④ wealth

◯ **Listening**　英文を聞いて理解しよう【知識・技能】【思考力・判断力・表現力】　　共通テスト　CD 17

Listen to the English and make the best choice to match the content. (4点)

   ① Rui Hachimura will have a game the next day.

   ② The speaker will see Hachimura in the arena.

   ③ The speaker will watch Hachimura's game on TV next week.

💬 **Interaction**　英文を聞いて会話を続けよう【知識・技能】【思考力・判断力・表現力】　スピーキング・トレーナー　CD 18

Listen to the English and respond to the last remark. (7点)

［メモ　　　　　　　　　　　　　　　　　　　　　　　　　　　　　　　　　　 ］

　アドバイス　質問されているわけではないが，相手の発言内容に対する自分の考えを述べよう。

✎ **Production（Write）**　自分の考えを書いて伝えよう【思考力・判断力・表現力】

Write your answer to the following question. (7点)

　　Have you learned about discrimination in school?

　アドバイス　Yes / No だけでなく，どんな内容だったかを記述しよう。

35

7 The history of the Olympics reminds us / of a well-known protest. // At the awards ceremony / for the 1968 Olympic Games / in Mexico City, / the first- and third-place winners / of the men's 200-meter track event, / both of whom were African-Americans / from the U.S., / looked down / and raised their **fists** / in black **gloves** / while the national anthem was being played. // This action was a protest / against the racial discrimination / in American society / at that time. // Such acts were **strictly** prohibited / by the Olympic **Charter**. // As a result, / they were sent back / to their country. //

8 The messages from athletes / have strong impacts / on society. // Their athletic performances and voices can encourage us / to become aware of / and more sensitive / to social issues. // As Rui says, / their performances can "inspire not only young players / in Japan / but also kids of mixed race / struggling with **racism**, / discrimination and identity issues." //

9 Racial discrimination can occur anywhere. // It is not limited / to the U.S., / and it should be considered / a clear **violation** / of human rights. // What is the message / you've gotten? // Athletes' actions send us messages, / just like Naomi wanted to send hers / to us. // (188 words)

🔊 **音読しよう**

Practice 1 　スラッシュ位置で文を区切って読んでみよう □

Practice 2 　イントネーションに注意して読んでみよう □

TRY! 　　　 １分50秒以内に本文全体を音読しよう □

スピーキング・トレーナー

📖 **Reading** 　本文の内容を読んで理解しよう【知識・技能】【思考力・判断力・表現力】　　　共通テスト

Make the correct choice to complete each sentence or answer each question. (各 4 点)

1. After the protest action at the ceremony in the 1968 Olympic Games, ☐ .

　① people in the U.S. welcomed them enthusiastically as heroes

　② people with sympathy took the same action all over the world

　③ the International Olympic Committee banned such actions

　④ the two medalists were sent back to the U.S.

2. According to Rui Hachimura, what can athletes' performances and voices do? ☐

　① They can encourage young players to come up to a global stage.

　② They can inspire children struggling with discrimination.

　③ They can make people more aware of social issues.

　④ They can solve racial discrimination.

3. One **fact** from paragraph 9 is that ☐ .

① athletes' actions send us messages　② Naomi Osaka sent her messages to us

③ racial discrimination can occur anywhere

④ racial discrimination should be considered a clear violation of human rights

🔍 Vocabulary & Grammar　重要表現や文法事項について理解しよう【知識】　英検® GTEC®

Make the correct choice to complete each sentence. (各2点)

1. The ski course was so steep that it was (　　　) to advanced skiers.

① abandoned　　② limited　　③ located　　④ unauthorized

2. Development of chemical and biological weapons is (　　　) prohibited.

① hopefully　　② immediately　　③ strictly　　④ urgently

3. The people living in the slum have long fought against (　　　).

① criticism　　② humanism　　③ racism　　④ sarcasm

4. After having crossed the border, they had to (　　　) with poverty.

① disagree　　② interact　　③ provide　　④ struggle

5. The company terminated the employee's contract due to a serious (　　　) of

company policies.

① application　　② innovation　　③ motivation　　④ violation

🎧 Listening　英文を聞いて理解しよう【知識・技能】【思考力・判断力・表現力】　共通テスト　CD 19

Listen to the English and make the best choice to match the content. (4点)

① Peter expressed his protest against wearing a badge.

② Peter is putting on a symbolic badge on his chest.

③ Peter protested against people's unfair behavior about race.

💬 Interaction　英文を聞いて会話を続けよう【知識・技能】【思考力・判断力・表現力】　スピーキング・トレーナー　CD 20

Listen to the English and respond to the last remark. (7点)

［メモ　　　　　　　　　　　　　　　　　　　　　　　　　　　　　　　　　　　　　　　］

アドバイス　social media は「SNS」の意味。

✍️ Production (Write)　自分の考えを書いて伝えよう【思考力・判断力・表現力】

Write your answer to the following question. (7点)

Do you know of any protest actions against discrimination?

アドバイス　人種差別に限らず，性別や年齢，障害の有無など，差別の種類は少なくありません。SNS での問題提起などもアクションの一つとなるでしょう。

You are learning / about the relationship / between the Olympics and human rights. // You found an article / about Rule 50 of the Olympic Charter. //

50: / Advertising, / demonstrations, / propaganda //

"No kind of demonstration / or political, **religious** / or racial propaganda / is permitted / in any Olympic sites, / **venues** or other areas." //

Why does this rule exist / and what does it aim / to achieve? //

The focus at the Olympic Games / must remain on athletes' performances, / sport / and the international **unity** / and harmony / that the Olympic Movement **seeks** / to advance. // Athletes at the Olympic Games / are part of a global community / with many different views, / lifestyles / and **values**. // The **mission** of the Olympic Games / to bring the entire world together / can **facilitate** the understanding / of different views, / but this can be accomplished / only if everybody respects / this **diversity**. //

Where are protests and demonstrations not permitted? //

At all Olympic venues, / including: /
   · On the field of play //
   · In the Olympic village //
   · During Olympic medal ceremonies //
   · During the opening, / closing and other official ceremonies //
● Any protest or demonstration / outside Olympic venues / must **comply** with local **legislation** / wherever local law **forbids** such actions. //

Where do athletes have the opportunity / to express their views? //

While respecting local laws, / athletes have the opportunity / to express their opinions, / including: /
   · During interviews //
   · At team meetings //
   · On digital / or traditional media //
● It should be noted / that expressing views / is different / from protesting and demonstrating. //

Here are some examples / of what would **constitute** a protest, / as **opposed** to expressing views: /
   · Displaying any political messages //
   · **Gestures** of a political nature / (Kneeling is permitted / before games.) //
   · **Refusal** to follow the ceremonies **protocol** //

(242 words)

◀)) 音読しよう   スピーキング・トレーナー

Practice 1   スラッシュ位置で文を区切って読んでみよう □
Practice 2   イントネーションに注意して読んでみよう □
TRY!   2分30秒以内に本文全体を音読しよう □

📖 Reading　本文の内容を読んで理解しよう【知識・技能】【思考力・判断力・表現力】　共通テスト

Make the correct choice to answer each question. (各6点)

1. What does "propaganda" mean in line 3? ☐
   ① truth　　　② conflict　　　③ publicity　　　④ technique
2. According to Rule 50, which of the following actions is **not** prohibited? ☐
   ① Expressing opinions at team meetings.
   ② Doing demonstration at the venue of the official ceremonies.
   ③ Holding up a sign of the political party the athlete supports.
   ④ Kneeling to express his/her protest during games.

🔍 Vocabulary & Grammar　重要表現や文法事項について理解しよう【知識】　英検 GTEC

Make the correct choice to complete each sentence. (各2点)

1. The advice was not something that they were (　　　).
   ① finding　　② holding　　③ owing　　④ seeking
2. Alcohol is strictly (　　　) in Islam.
   ① encouraged　② forbidden　③ preserved　④ struggled
3. Their refusal to (　　　) with the emperor's order led to another war.
   ① comply　　② dissent　　③ react　　④ start
4. Susan likes to collect artworks and appreciates the (　　　) of them.
   ① benefit　　② method　　③ notion　　④ value
5. My car was (　　　) when I passed the car repairer.
   ① be fixed　② been fixed　③ being fixed　④ fixed

🎧 Listening　英文を聞いて理解しよう【知識・技能】【思考力・判断力・表現力】　共通テスト　CD 21

Listen to the English and make the best choice to match the content. (各6点)

1. When were the new guidelines published?
   ① About a few months before the Olympic Games.
   ② About three days before the Olympic Games.
   ③ About twenty days before the Olympic Games.
   ④ About two weeks before the Olympic Games.
2. Which national teams kneeled the same way as Great Britain?
   ① Chili and Japan did.　　　② New Zealand and Australia did.
   ③ Sweden and Brazil did.　　④ U.S.A. and Germany did.
3. Which of the following is true about Stephanie Houghton?
   ① Her team followed the kneeling of another team.
   ② Her team showed an ethnic flag before the game.
   ③ She protested against the IOC's guidelines.
   ④ She represented a national soccer team.

Babies are often described / as "**linguistic geniuses**," / but we do not fully understand / the process of their language **acquisition** / or the challenges / they face. // Can you get any hints / for your learning / of English? //

① Do you remember / how you learned / your first language? // Probably none of you do. // Even so, / you may think / that babies master their first language, / or mother tongue, / with little difficulty. // Is that true? // Research findings from **infant** studies / suggest that babies, / **despite** their **talent**, / need much time and effort / to master language. //

② Language acquisition begins / when babies start / to **perceive** sounds. // More **precisely**, / they first need / to become aware / that people around them use language / to communicate with each other. // Babies are then required / to identify words / (for example, / "milk") / from a **series** of **unfamiliar** sounds / (for example, / [dʒúːwάntsəmmílk]) / to understand / what people are saying. // It may be surprising / to know / that most babies seem / to develop this ability / by the age of eight months. //

③ Babies do not learn language / by themselves; / assistance from people / around them / is essential / for their language development. // For example, / **caregivers** often use a clearer, **simplified** form / of speech / called "baby talk" / to interact with small children. // A **large-scale** study / **conducted** across cultures and continents / has shown that babies respond better / to baby talk / than to normal adult speech. // (189 words)

🔊 **音読しよう**　　　　　　　　　　　　　　　　　　　スピーキング・トレーナー
Practice 1　スラッシュ位置で文を区切って読んでみよう ☐
Practice 2　イントネーションに注意して読んでみよう ☐
TRY!　　　　1分50秒以内に本文全体を音読しよう ☐

📖 **Reading**　本文の内容を読んで理解しよう【知識・技能】【思考力・判断力・表現力】　　共通テスト

Make the correct choice to complete each sentence or answer each question. (各4点)

1. Language acquisition begins when babies ☐ .
   ① are born
   ② become aware that language is used for human communication
   ③ become the age of eight months　　④ learn to identify words

2. Which of the following is **not** true about "baby talk"? ☐
   ① A large-scale study about it has been conducted all around the world.
   ② Babies respond better to it than to normal adult speech.
   ③ It is a clearer and simplified language to interact with small children.
   ④ It is the first language that babies learn by themselves.

3. According to the paragraphs, _____.

① babies have abilities to develop their language skills by themselves

② babies learn language with little difficulty

③ babies start to identify words by the age of eight month

④ "baby talk" may spoil babies' language developing skills

🔍 **Vocabulary & Grammar**　重要表現や文法事項について理解しよう【知識】　　英検® GTEC®

Make the correct choice to complete each sentence. (各2点)

1. The Alaska Purchase was the United States' (　　　) of Alaska from the Russian Empire in 1867.

① acquisition　　② construction　　③ possession　　④ translation

2. My vacation was a lot of fun, (　　　) the weather.

① although　　② but　　③ despite　　④ regardless

3. Elections have been fairly (　　　) since the foundation of the country.

① conducted　　② demanded　　③ manipulated　　④ stimulated

4. Akira shows up (　　　) at eight every morning.

① certainly　　② frequently　　③ precisely　　④ strictly

5. A (　　　) of phone calls prevented Meg from concentrating on her writing.

① cycles　　② lines　　③ row　　④ series

🎧 **Listening**　英文を聞いて理解しよう【知識・技能】【思考力・判断力・表現力】　共通テスト　CD 22

Listen to the English and make the best choice to match the content. (4点)

① It has been seven months since the baby was born.

② The baby is half a year old now.

③ The speaker talks to the baby to wake him up.

💬 **Interaction**　英文を聞いて会話を続けよう【知識・技能】【思考力・判断力・表現力】　スピーキング・トレーナー　CD 23

Listen to the English and respond to the last remark. (7点)

［メモ　　　　　　　　　　　　　　　　　　　　　　　　　　　　　　　　　　　　　　　 ］

アドバイス　相手の発言と同様に，必ず理由を付け加えよう。

💬 **Production (Speak)**　自分の考えを話して伝えよう【思考力・判断力・表現力】　スピーキング・トレーナー

Speak out your answer to the following question. (7点)

What activities or lessons do you want your children to learn when you become a parent? Why?

アドバイス　理由がしっかり論理的であるかに注意しよう。

------

④ Just like with speech **perception**, / babies need / to pass through a number of stages / as they learn to talk. // From birth, / babies make a range of noises / such as crying and **coughing**. // They then start / to make **cooing** noises / like "ooh" and "aah." // By six to nine months, / they begin / to enjoy repeating certain sounds / such as "dada" and "gaga" / over and over / again. // This is commonly called "**babbling**." //

⑤ It is only after babies turn 12 months old / that they finally begin / to say a few simple words / such as "**mama**" and "mum." // Their **vocabulary** continues / to grow **afterwards**, / reaching about 200 words / in total / at around the age of 24 months. // Some babies are said / to experience a sudden growth / in their vocabulary / between 18 and 24 months of age. // This is called a "vocabulary **spurt**." //

⑥ Babies also learn to point at things / when they are between 12 and 18 months old. // Pointing is an essential tool / for their early communication / to show their **desires** / and draw attention, / especially when they cannot yet express themselves / well / in words. // After having **elicited reactions** / from others, / babies often begin to say a word / for something / that they have pointed to / previously. // (200 words)

🔊 **音読しよう**
Practice 1　スラッシュ位置で文を区切って読んでみよう ☐
Practice 2　イントネーションに注意して読んでみよう ☐
TRY!　　　2分以内に本文全体を音読しよう ☐

スピーキング・トレーナー

📖 **Reading**　本文の内容を読んで理解しよう【知識・技能】【思考力・判断力・表現力】　共通テスト

Make the correct choice to complete each sentence or answer each question. (各4点)

1. Put the events in the order they occurred. ☐ → ☐ → ☐ → ☐

　① Babies begin to say a few simple words such as "mama" and "mum."

　② Babies make noises such as crying and coughing.

　③ Babies repeat certain sounds such as "dada" and "gaga."

　④ Babies start making cooing noises like "ooh" and "aah."

2. "Vocabulary spurt" is ☐.

　① not precisely defined among experts

　② seen in almost all babies aged between 18 and 24 months

　③ seen in children between 18 and 24 months acquiring new words

　④ when a baby's vocabulary reaches about 200 words

3. According to paragraph 6, when do babies start pointing at things? ☐

　① Around six to nine months old.　　② Around the age of 24 months old.

　③ Between 12 and 18 months old.　　④ Between 18 and 24 months old.

🔍 Vocabulary & Grammar   重要表現や文法事項について理解しよう【知識】   英検® GTEC®

Make the correct choice to complete each sentence. (各2点)

1. XYZ mobile company provides a (　　　) of options for this service.

   ① heap   ② piece   ③ range   ④ touch

2. The butterfly was flying quickly, as if trying to (　　　) my attention.

   ① concentrate   ② draw   ③ pay   ④ turn

3. The photographer told jokes or used funny faces to (　　　) a natural smile from children.

   ① conduct   ② elicit   ③ grant   ④ represent

4. Sarah had a strong (　　　) to travel the world and experience different cultures.

   ① desire   ② fear   ③ happiness   ④ talent

5. We're often surprised by a child's (　　　) of family issues.

   ① appreciation   ② innovation   ③ perception   ④ restriction

🎧 Listening   英文を聞いて理解しよう【知識・技能】【思考力・判断力・表現力】   共通テスト   CD 24

Listen to the English and make the best choice to match the content. (4点)

　① The baby looked at the dog.

　② The baby pointed at the speaker.

　③ The speaker smiled at the baby.

💬 Interaction   英文を聞いて会話を続けよう【知識・技能】【思考力・判断力・表現力】   スピーキング・トレーナー   CD 25

Listen to the English and respond to the last remark. (7点)

　［メモ　　］

　アドバイス 何か相手にアドバイスとなるような情報を伝える。

✏️ Production (Write)   自分の考えを書いて伝えよう【思考力・判断力・表現力】

Write your answer to the following question. (7点)

　If it were not for language, how would you communicate with your friends?

　アドバイス どのように自分の考えを相手に伝えるか，考えてみよう。

⑦ Some of you may hope / to raise children / with good **bilingual** skills, / but that can be **challenging**. // This is because a baby's brain is naturally **adapted** / to its environment. // When **exposed** only to Japanese, / newly-born babies become good / at understanding Japanese. // On the other hand, / they will eventually stop distinguishing sounds / such as /l/ and /r/, / which are important to English / but not to Japanese. // Balancing two languages is a very difficult task. //

⑧ American **psychologist** Patricia Kuhl and her **colleagues** / **examined** whether English-speaking infants could maintain / their ability / to tell **apart** two Mandarin sounds. // Interestingly, / they found / that babies who **engaged** in **interaction** / with an actual Mandarin-speaking person / were more likely to maintain / this ability / than others who listened only to Mandarin sounds / from non-**interactive** audio recordings. // Babies seem / to find interaction more **meaningful** and **relevant** / to their lives. // This could have a positive influence / on their language development. //

⑨ These findings suggest / that babies develop their language skills / in order to communicate with people / around them. // Whether it is a first / or a second language, / such motivation drives our language development. // What about your learning / of English? // Who would you like to interact with? // Little babies may be offering us / a good chance / to reflect on our own language learning. // (210 words)

🔊 **音読しよう**　　　　　　　　　　　　　　スピーキング・トレーナー
Practice 1　スラッシュ位置で文を区切って読んでみよう □
Practice 2　イントネーションに注意して読んでみよう □
TRY!　　　　2分10秒以内に本文全体を音読しよう □

📖 **Reading**　本文の内容を読んで理解しよう【知識・技能】【思考力・判断力・表現力】　　共通テスト

Make the correct choice to complete each sentence or answer each question. (各4点)

1. Babies who interacted with an actual Mandarin-speaking person could ⬚.

　① find a positive influence on their language development

　② maintain their ability to tell apart two Mandarin sounds

　③ maintain their ability to tell apart two Mandarin sounds as those who listened to them from audio recordings

　④ not maintain their ability to tell apart two Mandarin sounds

2. Which of the following is **not** true about language development? ⬚

　① Babies acquire language through communication with people around them.

　② Becoming bilingual is not easy task even for babies.

　③ Interacting with people may help your language acquisition.

　④ Listening to audio recordings can effectively develop our language skills.

3.　Which of the following has the same meaning as "distinguish" in line 5?　☐
　① engage in　　　② maintain　　　③ reflect　　　④ tell apart

🔍 Vocabulary & Grammar　重要表現や文法事項について理解しよう【知識】　英検® GTEC®

Make the correct choice to complete each sentence. (各2点)

1.　The photograph was spotted after being (　　　) to moisture.
　① covered　　　② exposed　　　③ protected　　　④ subjected
2.　Half of the world's population (　　　) in agriculture.
　① engages　　　② faces　　　③ keeps　　　④ results
3.　It took some time for him to (　　　) to living in a large city.
　① accept　　　② adapt　　　③ adjust　　　④ adopt
4.　I didn't know how to deal with competitive (　　　) in my previous job.
　① colleagues　　　② infants　　　③ neighbors　　　④ supporters
5.　In this presentation, the speaker discussed various topics that were (　　　) to the theme of environmental sustainability.
　① apart　　　② challenging　　　③ interactive　　　④ relevant

◯ Listening　英文を聞いて理解しよう【知識・技能】【思考力・判断力・表現力】　共通テスト CD 26

Listen to the English and make the best choice to match the content. (4点)
　① Mike can probably speak both Italian and English very well.
　② Mike probably doesn't have good English-language skills.
　③ Mike probably isn't good at speaking Japanese.

💬 Interaction　英文を聞いて会話を続けよう【知識・技能】【思考力・判断力・表現力】　スピーキング・トレーナー CD 27

Listen to the English and respond to the last remark. (7点)
　［メ モ　　　　　　　　　　　　　　　　　　　　　　　　　　　　　　　　　　］
　アドバイス　発音がよいメリットは何か考えてみよう。

✎ Production (Write)　自分の考えを書いて伝えよう【思考力・判断力・表現力】

Write your answer to the following question. (7点)
　Do you think we need to learn foreign languages in the age of AI translation?
　アドバイス　機械翻訳の精度があがっていくことでできること，できないことを考えてみよう。

A researcher visits a high school / to give a short **lecture** / on how to find out / what babies know / or are thinking. // Here is the **script** / of his lecture. //

Babies cannot explain their understanding / in words. // Do you know / how researchers **investigate** their knowledge? // Today, / I will talk / about some popular methods / used in baby studies. //

The first method is called a **preferential** looking test, / which is often used / to determine babies' favorite things. // Babies tend to look longer / at things / or sources of sounds / they like. // In an **experiment**, / for example, / a baby sits on its parent's **lap** / in a small room, / with a light **bulb** / on each of the left / and right walls. // **Loudspeakers** are built / in behind each light. // Once the child looks at one of the lights, / a speech **stream** is played. // Of course, / each loudspeaker plays a different sound. // By measuring the looking time, / we can investigate babies' preference. // I mean, / the longer they look, / the better they like the sound. //

Another common method is a **habituation-dishabituation** test. // Babies tend to express interest / in something new, / so we make use of this **tendency** / when doing an experiment. // For example, / when a baby is exposed **repeatedly** / to a certain sound, / the baby gets bored / with it / and eventually no longer looks at the source / of the sound. // This is called a habituation. // Then, / a different sound is played. // If the baby can distinguish the sounds, / it should look again / at the loudspeaker / because, / as I said, / babies like something new. // This "dishabituation" does not occur / if a baby cannot tell the difference / between the two sounds. //

What other methods / do you think we can use? // Some researchers create a special **pacifier**, / which plays a sound / only when babies suck hard. // Others use an eye **tracker** / to **detect** babies' eye positions / and movements. // As I explained / today, / we need appropriate methods / and techniques / to design **reputable** baby studies. // **Creativity** is one of the keys / we need to use / to **unlock** the **mysteries** of / how babies develop. // Can you come up with any other good methods? // (319 words)

🔊 **音読しよう**

Practice 1　スラッシュ位置で文を区切って読んでみよう☐

Practice 2　イントネーションに注意して読んでみよう☐

TRY!　3分10秒以内に本文全体を音読しよう☐

スピーキング・トレーナー

📖 **Reading**　本文の内容を読んで理解しよう【知識・技能】【思考力・判断力・表現力】　　共通テスト

Make the correct choice to complete each sentence or answer each question. (各7点)

1. A preferential looking test makes use of the characteristic that babies look in the direction of what they ☐.

① afford　　　　② like　　　　③ hate　　　　④ hear

2. Which of the following is used to test a baby's ability to distinguish two sounds?

① A preferential looking test　　　② A habituation-dishabituation test

③ A test using a special pacifier　　④ A test using an eye tracker

🔍 Vocabulary & Grammar　重要表現や文法事項について理解しよう【知識】　英検® GTEC®

Make the correct choice to complete each sentence. (各2点)

1. Make sure that you are making your purchase from (　　) companies.
   ① available　　② edible　　③ reputable　　④ visible

2. The police chief ordered his team to continue to (　　) the case.
   ① evacuate　　② facilitate　　③ investigate　　④ stimulate

3. How can he always (　　) with such brilliant ideas?
   ① come up　　② get along　　③ keep up　　④ put up

4. Using mice in scientific (　　) is still common.
   ① demonstrations　② experiments　③ presentations　④ rehearsals

5. After a few mornings in the hotel, we got (　　) with the selection of foods.
   ① bored　　② excited　　③ upset　　④ satisfied

6. The blood test may be able to (　　) cancer.
   ① confess　　② detect　　③ prove　　④ signify

7. Using your imagination and (　　) is the best way to start your business.
   ① announcement　② creativity　③ hesitation　④ security

🎧 Listening　英文を聞いて理解しよう【知識・技能】【思考力・判断力・表現力】　共通テスト CD 28

Listen to the English and make the best choice to match the content. (各4点)

1. What month was the speaker's daughter born?
   ① February　　② March　　③ April　　④ May

2. Why did the speaker think about the time before her daughter was born?
   ① Because her daughter kicked her from inside.
   ② Because her daughter talked to her.
   ③ Because she interviewed a researcher about the experiment.
   ④ Because she read an article on the Internet.

3. What did the researcher examine about unborn babies?
   ① The shape of their hearts　　　② The size of their feet
   ③ The sounds they make　　　　　④ Their movements

47

What does it mean / to "go digital"? // How will the digital age continue / to develop, / and how will it impact us / and our society? //

① What does the word "digital" bring to mind? // Some may think / of smartphones, / personal computers / and tablets. // Others may imagine / e-books, / streaming music, / and online video games. // These are all **electronic**, / not quite physical, / and this is one of the important **aspects** / of going digital. //

② **Digitization** refers to the process of changing information / into an electronic **format** / that can be read / and processed / by a computer. // A smartphone, / for example, / can work / as a map, / a book / and a watch. // These things previously existed / as separate physical items, / but now / their contents and functions / have been changed / into digital formats / — apps. //

③ So, / what happens / when information is **digitized**? // Take the example / of digitized **documents**. // Digitized documents can go **beyond** space / and time **limitations**. // As they have no physical **presence**, / they no longer need physical space / for storage. // They are easier / to **edit** or copy, / and any edits can be easily **undone**. // Furthermore, / digitized information can more **readily** be connected / online. // These properties can help / make the process and state of things / **visible** and **manageable** / **virtually** / **anytime** and anywhere. // (179 words)

🔊 **音読しよう**
　スピーキング・トレーナー

Practice 1　スラッシュ位置で文を区切って読んでみよう☐
Practice 2　イントネーションに注意して読んでみよう☐
TRY!　　　　1分50秒以内に本文全体を音読しよう☐

📖 **Reading**　本文の内容を読んで理解しよう【知識・技能】【思考力・判断力・表現力】　共通テスト

Make the correct choice to answer each question. (各4点)

1. According to paragraph 1, which of the following is one of the important aspects of going digital? ☐
   ① Being electronic.　　　　　　　② Doing physical activities.
   ③ Enjoying e-books, streaming music, and online video games.
   ④ Having smartphones, personal computers and tablets.

2. Which of the following is the digital form of something that originally existed physically? ☐
   ① AI　　　　　② Apps　　　　　③ IoT　　　　　④ Social media

● イントネーションを理解して音読することができる。　　　📖 デジタイゼーションに関する英文を読んで，概要や要点を捉えることができる。
🔍 文脈を理解して適切な語句を用いて英文を完成することができる。　　🎧 平易な英語で話される短い英文を聞いて必要な情報を聞き取ることができる。
💬 オンラインでの行動について簡単な語句を用いて説明できる。　　💬 デジタル化について簡単な語句を用いて考えを表現することができる。

Goals

3. Which of the following does **not** happen when information is digitized? ☐

① Documents take physical space for storage.

② Documents are easily edited, copied and undone.

③ Documents can readily be connected online.

④ Documents become visible and manageable anytime and anywhere.

🔍 Vocabulary & Grammar　重要表現や文法事項について理解しよう【知識】　　英検® GTEC®

Make the correct choice to complete each sentence. (各2点)

1. What are the positive (　　　) of living alone for you?

　① aspects　　　　② findings　　　　③ reasons　　　　④ views

2. The new coach's role of the team did not go (　　　) just giving advice.

　① ahead　　　　② beyond　　　　③ over　　　　④ under

3. Tokyo Skytree is (　　　) from the building on a clear day.

　① accessible　　② horrible　　　③ impossible　　④ visible

4. The scent of the flower (　　　) to mind a tropical place.

　① brought　　　② carried　　　③ got　　　　④ traveled

5. I don't know what I just did on my PC …. Someone, tell me how to (　　　) it!

　① do　　　　　② overdo　　　　③ redo　　　　④ undo

🎧 Listening　英文を聞いて理解しよう【知識・技能】【思考力・判断力・表現力】　　共通テスト　CD 29

Listen to the English and make the best choice to match the content. (4点)

① The speaker agrees to stop buying traditional newspapers.

② The speaker thinks electric newspapers are harder to read than paper ones.

③ The speaker wants to cut more costs on electricity.

💬 Interaction　英文を聞いて会話を続けよう【知識・技能】【思考力・判断力・表現力】　スピーキング・トレーナー　CD 30

Listen to the English and respond to the last remark. (7点)

[メモ　　　　　　　　　　　　　　　　　　　　　　　　　　　　　　　　　　　　　]

アドバイス　相手と同じことをしているという回答でも OK です。

💬 Production (Speak)　自分の考えを話して伝えよう【思考力・判断力・表現力】　スピーキング・トレーナー

Speak out your answer to the following question. (7点)

Do you think all of your letters from school should be distributed online? Why or why not?

アドバイス　学校の配布物をデジタル化すべきかどうかという問いです。自分の考えを明確に示そう。

- -

- -

④ Digitization concerns changing something / into digital data, / but "**digitalization**" takes things / a step further. // Making use of digital data / and the abilities of various recent technologies, / digitalization entirely changes the process / of doing things. // It **involves** collecting / and analyzing data, / running **simulations** / and making better decisions / about what to do. //

⑤ One of the key **digitalized** technologies / is the Internet of Things (IoT). // It allows physical **objects** / to be connected / online. // These objects are **equipped** / with sensors, / cameras, / and other technologies / that help connect / and exchange data / with other devices and systems. // Cloud technology can remove data storage limitations. // Also, / AI technologies make it possible / to run **precise** simulations / based on collected data. //

⑥ An example of digitalization is / the use of a digital **twin**. // It is a **virtual replica** / of a physical thing, / which can display / what the real one is doing / or is going to do. // This technology was **employed** / in the 2018 FIFA World Cup. // In each match, / the player and ball movements / were tracked / in real time / and were **reproduced** / **digitally**. // The participating teams were allowed / to use the **analysis** / and simulation results / for their decision-making / during the match. //

(191 words)

🔊 **音読しよう**

スピーキング・トレーナー

Practice 1 スラッシュ位置で文を区切って読んでみよう ☐
Practice 2 イントネーションに注意して読んでみよう ☐
TRY! 1分50秒以内に本文全体を音読しよう ☐

📖 **Reading** 本文の内容を読んで理解しよう【知識・技能】【思考力・判断力・表現力】 共通テスト

Make the correct choice to complete each sentence or answer each question. (各4点)

1. Which of the following is **not** an example of "digitalization"? ☐
   ① A bookstore started e-commerce using the analysis of big data.
   ② A supermarket uses an AI system that automatically purchases products based on consumer preferences.
   ③ A company conducts the survey online and analyzes it automatically.
   ④ You read books on your e-reader.

2. According to paragraph 5, cloud technology helps ☐ .
   ① remove data storage limitations
   ② run precise simulations based on collected data
   ③ sensors, cameras and other technologies be removed
   ④ weather forecast be more accurate

3. "A digital twin" was used in the 2018 FIFA World Cup to ⬚ .

① choose players to be employed to work for FIFA

② display the actual game from various viewpoints

③ make a replica of the players' unforms

④ track the movements of the players and ball

🔍 Vocabulary & Grammar　重要表現や文法事項について理解しよう【知識】　英検® GTEC®

Make the correct choice to complete each sentence. (各2点)

1. The new theater is (　　) with the latest audio systems.
　① content　　② equipped　　③ organized　　④ wrapped

2. You can set the (　　) temperature with the remote controller.
　① rough　　② crucial　　③ precise　　④ significant

3. An unidentified (　　) entered the country's airspace last night.
　① contact　　② item　　③ object　　④ subject

4. A decision like that should (　　) the manager.
　① convince　　② involve　　③ persuade　　④ update

5. He found a job in which he can (　　) his considerable writing skills.
　① employ　　② hire　　③ pretend　　④ remark

🎧 Listening　英文を聞いて理解しよう【知識・技能】【思考力・判断力・表現力】　共通テスト CD 31

Listen to the English and make the best choice to match the content. (4点)

① The speaker explains how to use an app.

② Users need a special machine to install an app.

③ With a special app, users can manage their smartphones.

🗨 Interaction　英文を聞いて会話を続けよう【知識・技能】【思考力・判断力・表現力】　スピーキング・トレーナー CD 32

Listen to the English and respond to the last remark. (7点)

［メモ　　　　　　　　　　　　　　　　　　　　　　　　　　　　　　　］

アドバイス　まず自分はどうか答えて，何か知っていることを付け加えよう。

✎ Production (Write)　自分の考えを書いて伝えよう【思考力・判断力・表現力】

Write your answer to the following question. (7点)

Which do you prefer, online class or face-to-face class? Explain your reasons.

アドバイス　両方にメリットがあるので，自分の考えにあう理由を考えよう。

⑦ When the use of digital technologies affects society / and human activity, / it is called "digital **transformation** (DX)." // In education, / for example, / DX may drastically change / how teaching and learning take place. // Students' learning data / is automatically collected / in digital form / all the time. // Based on that information, / the most suitable study content / and plans / can be suggested, / enabling both teachers and learners / to create a more effective / and engaging **educational** process. //

⑧ DX also impacts the notion / of shopping / and our behavior / as consumers. // Online shopping has brought about virtual shopping. // **Personalized recommendations** / on a shopping website / constitute the digitalization / of what a **salesclerk** used to do / in the physical shop. // The lines / between digital and in-store shopping experiences / are becoming less clear / than they were / before. //

⑨ Promoting digitization, / digitalization / or digital transformation / is not necessarily easy, / however. // In the business world, / companies and organizations cannot **afford** / to provide training / for their **employees** / to cover all of the necessary digital skills. // **Transforming** the existing systems / into digital ones / could be heavily **constrained** / if they are too **complex** / and are already "black boxes." // Still, / going digital seems / to be an **inevitable** trend. // How far are we now / from a fully digital world? // (200 words)

🔊 **音読しよう**

Practice 1 スラッシュ位置で文を区切って読んでみよう ☐
Practice 2 イントネーションに注意して読んでみよう ☐
TRY! 2分以内に本文全体を音読しよう ☐

スピーキング・トレーナー

📖 **Reading** 本文の内容を読んで理解しよう【知識・技能】【思考力・判断力・表現力】 共通テスト

Make the correct choice to complete each sentence or answer each question. (各4点)

1. "Digital transformation (DX)" is the use of digital technologies that ☐.

   ① affects society and human activity

   ② changes the roles of teachers

   ③ collects students' learning data all the time

   ④ brings a salesclerk anytime you want

2. Which of the following is **not** mentioned as an example of DX? ☐

   ① Personalized recommendations show on a shopping website.

   ② The existing systems are transformed into digital ones in businesses.

   ③ The item that you ordered online is trackable in a timely manner.

   ④ The most suitable study content and plans are suggested to each student.

3. According to the paragraphs, "going digital" is ☐.
① a "black box"　　　　　② easy
③ inevitable　　　　　　④ not necessary

🔍 **Vocabulary & Grammar**　重要表現や文法事項について理解しよう【知識】　英検® GTEC®

Make the correct choice to complete each sentence.（各2点）

1. His aim was to (　　) about peace to the devastated land.
① bring　　　② care　　　③ think　　　④ worry

2. The museum offers a variety of interactive exhibits that provide (　　) experience for visitors.
① an educational　② a commercial　③ a institutional　④ a traditional

3. I can't (　　) to buy a car and pay insurance.
① afford　　　② deal　　　③ handle　　　④ stand

4. As natural disasters seem (　　), we need to prepare for them.
① avoidable　② incredible　③ inevitable　④ responsible

5. I asked my friend for a book (　　) because I wanted to find a new novel to read.
① occasion　　② passion　　③ recommendation　④ preference

🎧 **Listening**　英文を聞いて理解しよう【知識・技能】【思考力・判断力・表現力】　共通テスト　CD 33

Listen to the English and make the best choice to match the content.（4点）
① Neither quizzes nor exams are given online.
② Students can choose either online or face-to-face quizzes.
③ Students can take online lessons only when they are sick.

💬 **Interaction**　英文を聞いて会話を続けよう【知識・技能】【思考力・判断力・表現力】　スピーキング・トレーナー　CD 34

Listen to the English and respond to the last remark.（7点）

［メ モ　　　　　　　　　　　　　　　　　　　　　　　　　　　　　　］

アドバイス ハンコを使う場面が身近にあるか考えて，自分の解答に付け加えよう。

✏ **Production（Write）**　自分の考えを書いて伝えよう【思考力・判断力・表現力】

Write your answer to the following question.（7点）

Which do you prefer, digital textbooks or printed ones?

アドバイス どちらにも多くのメリットがある。それらを踏まえて自分の意見を述べよう。

You are looking for some information / about going **paperless** / on the Internet / and have found the following blog post / about the positive aspects / of paper use. //

Going paperless will bring us / a lot of benefits. // However, / that doesn't mean / we should stop using paper / completely. // There seem to be positive aspects / of paper / that should be noted. //

First of all, / paper is simple / and easy to use. // Even a small child can understand / how to use it. // Also, / paper does not require devices / or electricity. // To use digital data, / some sort of digital device, / such as a computer / or a tablet, / is a must. // Without an electronic device, / digital data can never be read / or created. //

Another good point about paper is / that it can be enjoyed / through the senses. // You can feel its **roughness** / or **smoothness** / and its smell. // If you write something / on it, / you can feel / its unique touch. // In these respects, / paper is more real / to us. // At present, / however, / it is impossible / for digital technology / to **replicate** / such experiences. //

Paper may be better / for your eyes, / particularly when you read / (or write) something / for a long time. // Due to their **brightness** / and glare, / digital screens can cause / more eye **strain** and fatigue / than reading / from a paper page. // For this reason, / there are definitely some people / who still **prefer** paper / to screen. //

Reading from paper can facilitate / better understanding / for the learner. // As it is friendly / to your eyes, / more time may be spent / on **concentrated** / and **in-depth** reading. // The **fatiguing** nature of digital on-screen reading / can lead / to non-linear **selective** reading, / which could **consequently** decrease / **sustained** attention / to the **text**. //

I believe / paper still holds an essential place / in this digital age / and is here / to stay. // (267 words)

◀)) **音読しよう**　　　　　　　　　　　　　　　　　　スピーキング・トレーナー

Practice 1　スラッシュ位置で文を区切って読んでみよう ☐
Practice 2　イントネーションに注意して読んでみよう ☐
TRY!　　　2分40秒以内に本文全体を音読しよう ☐

📖 **Reading**　本文の内容を読んで理解しよう【知識・技能】【思考力・判断力・表現力】　　　共通テスト

Make the correct choice to complete each sentence or answer each question. (各6点)

1. One **fact** about paper use is that ☐ .

① it does not require devices or electricity

② it can be enjoyed through the senses

③ more time may be spent on reading

④ it still holds an essential place in this digital age

2. What does "facilitate" mean in line 20? ☐

① assist 　　　　　② cease 　　　　　③ hinder 　　　　　④ translate

Vocabulary & Grammar　重要表現や文法事項について理解しよう【知識】　英検 ® GTEC ®

Make the correct choice to complete each sentence. (各2点)

1. About 400 species of sharks are recognized at (　　　).

① all 　　　　　② last 　　　　　③ once 　　　　　④ present

2. Do cats (　　　) to be alone to have companies of other cats?

① aim 　　　　　② like 　　　　　③ prefer 　　　　　④ stay

3. I closed my eyes to (　　　) hard on my study.

① concentrate 　　② complete 　　③ consider 　　④ contribute

4. The researcher takes an (　　　), highly practical approach in her study.

① all-inclusive 　　② in-depth 　　③ off-campus 　　④ on-screen

5. Their long and (　　　) worldwide tour has finally finished.

① convincing 　　② fatiguing 　　③ involving 　　④ reminding

6. Carrying heavy backpacks can lead to back (　　　).

① ease 　　　　　② press 　　　　　③ relief 　　　　　④ strain

7. Many fashion designers around the world (　　　) European fashion today.

① advocate 　　② donate 　　③ replicate 　　④ translate

8. My mother has to get up early (　　　) she can catch the first bus.

① for fear that 　　② in case 　　③ otherwise 　　④ so that

Listening　英文を聞いて理解しよう【知識・技能】【思考力・判断力・表現力】　共通テスト　CD 35

Listen to the English and make the best choice to match the content. (各4点)

1. What does the speaker mind?

① An increase in the number of bankbooks.

② Going to the ATM many times.

③ Switching to the digital bankbook.

④ The ATM crowded with people.

2. How many bankbooks does the speaker have?

① Four 　　　② Five 　　　③ Six 　　　④ Seven

3. Which of the following is true about the speaker's digital bankbook?

① He can find a record of three years ago.

② He can't use it yet.

③ He has to update it regularly.

④ He will make a digital document once a day.

Some of you may remember / the year 2020 / as a bad one / for public health. // When looking into our past, / we realize / that people in the past experienced / similar health crises. // They might have had the same feelings / as you did. //

① The World Health Organization, / or WHO, / **declared** the COVID-19 **infections** / a **pandemic** / on March 12, 2020. // In fact, / this was not the first time / that human beings **combatted** / infectious diseases / on a global stage. // We have a very long history / of fighting against them. // With changes / in the global environment / and human behavior, / various diseases and sicknesses have come / and gone. //

② Infectious diseases are illnesses / caused by **microorganisms** / such as bacteria, / **viruses** / or **parasites**. // Many of them / live in and on our bodies, / and are normally **harmless** / or sometimes even beneficial. // Under certain conditions, / however, / some **organisms** may cause diseases. // Bacteria are **relatively** complex, / single-**cell** creatures, / and they can reproduce / on their own. // In contrast, / a virus cannot survive / without a host. // It is always looking for a place / to leave its **offspring**. // When a virus enters the human body / and reproduces, / it causes **harm**. //

③ People have been fighting / against infectious diseases / since ancient times. // According to some researchers, / examinations of **Egyptian mummies** / have shown / that those people suffered / from various diseases / and parasites. // As one example, / the eggs of disease-carrying parasites / that came from eating **snails** / were found / in some mummies. // (192 words)

◀))) 音読しよう　　　　　　　　　　　　　　スピーキング・トレーナー
Practice 1　スラッシュ位置で文を区切って読んでみよう ☐
Practice 2　音の変化に注意して読んでみよう ☐
TRY!　　　　2分以内に本文全体を音読しよう ☐

📖 **Reading**　本文の内容を読んで理解しよう【知識・技能】【思考力・判断力・表現力】　　共通テスト

Make the correct choice to complete each sentence or answer each question. (各4点)

1. Which of the following is **not** true about COVID-19? ☐
   ① It has caused changes in the global environment and in human behavior.
   ② It was one of the various diseases and sicknesses that we needed to fight against.
   ③ It was the first infectious disease that human beings combatted on a global stage.
   ④ The World Health Organization declared it a pandemic on March 12, 2020.

2. Which of the following phrases refers to 'a host' in line 15? ☐
   ① Bacteria, viruses or parasites　　② Infectious diseases
   ③ Its offspring　　　　　　　　　④ The human body

◀) 音の変化を理解して音読することができる。	📖 病気の原因に関する英文を読んで，概要や要点を捉えることができる。
🔍 文脈を理解して適切な語句を用いて英文を完成することができる。	🎧 平易な英語で話される短い英文を聞いて必要な情報を聞き取ることができる。
💬 体調について簡単な語句を用いてコメントすることができる。	💬 リモートワークについて簡単な語句を用いて考えを表現することができる。

Goals

3. Examinations of Egyptian mummies have shown that ⬚.

① the ancient Egyptians had changed the environment and their behavior

② the ancient Egyptians knew what caused their diseases

③ the ancient Egyptians suffered from various diseases and parasites

④ there were times of hunger when the ancient Egyptians had to eat snails

🔍 Vocabulary & Grammar　重要表現や文法事項について理解しよう【知識】　英検® GTEC®

Make the correct choice to complete each sentence. (各2点)

1. The doctor told me that the (　　　) had spread to the other lung.

① diagnosis 　　② infection 　　③ phenomenon 　　④ oxgen

2. The product was recalled due to potential (　　) to consumers.

① advantage 　　② benefit 　　③ harm 　　④ improvement

3. The mother lion carefully protected her newborn (　　) from any potential threats.

① ancestors 　　② offspring 　　③ siblings 　　④ spectators

4. In large airports, people could (　　) at all hours.

① catch and release 　② come and go 　　③ hit and run 　　④ park and ride

5. She has (　　) for a call from the company for almost an hour.

① been waited 　　② been waiting 　　③ waited 　　④ waiting

🎧 Listening　英文を聞いて理解しよう【知識・技能】【思考力・判断力・表現力】　共通テスト　CD 36

Listen to the English and make the best choice to match the content. (4点)

① Some patients ended up dying within a few months.

② The bacteria caused about three of every ten patients to die.

③ The virus was strong enough to kill some patients.

💬 Interaction　英文を聞いて会話を続けよう【知識・技能】【思考力・判断力・表現力】　スピーキング・トレーナー　CD 37

Listen to the English and respond to the last remark. (7点)

[メモ 　　　　　　　　　　　　　　　　　　　　　　　　　　　　　　　　]

アドバイス　相手の体調を気遣うコメントをしてあげよう。

💬 Production (Speak)　自分の考えを話して伝えよう【思考力・判断力・表現力】　スピーキング・トレーナー

Speak out your answer to the following question. (7点)

Do you prefer to work from home or in the office when you start a job?

アドバイス　コロナ禍ではリモートワーク実施企業が増えた。自分はどちらが好きか理由とともに答えよう。

④ Infectious diseases are mirrors of the times / —— they have changed their forms / according to people's lifestyles / of the time. // When the earliest humans began to **settle** / on **riversides**, / sharing the river water / caused **epidemics** / of **digestive** diseases. // When people started / to gather / in cities / and live closer together, / illnesses could be **transmitted** / more easily / from person to person. // When cities became larger, / there were no sewage systems / in the beginning, / and diseases spread / through human waste. //

⑤ In response to the spread of diseases, / people have transformed / social systems. // In big cities / of Europe / in the 14th century, / a large number of rats / spread the **plague** bacteria. // This plague pandemic was responsible / for killing an estimated 60 percent / of Europe's entire population. // The spread of the disease / caused the social structure / to change **significantly**, / which, / on the bright side, / led to the **liberation** / of people / and the **Renaissance** era. //

⑥ Four centuries later / during the **Industrial Revolution**, / many factories were built / and people migrated / from rural areas / to cities / to work. // They had to work hard / and were poorly nourished, / which made many of them sick. // **Tuberculosis** soon became epidemic. // Protesting against their bad working conditions, / many workers, / including children, / set up unions / and fought against their **employers**. // They succeeded / in improving their working and living conditions. // (216 words)

🔊 **音読しよう**　　　　　　　　　　　　　　　スピーキング・トレーナー
Practice 1　スラッシュ位置で文を区切って読んでみよう ☐
Practice 2　音の変化に注意して読んでみよう ☐
TRY!　　　2分10秒以内に本文全体を音読しよう ☐

📖 **Reading**　本文の内容を読んで理解しよう【知識・技能】【思考力・判断力・表現力】　　共通テスト

Make the correct choice to complete each sentence or answer each question. (各4点)

1. Why are infectious diseases "mirrors of the times"? ☐
   ① Because becoming sick shows who you really are.
   ② Because humans used the surface of the river as a mirror to reflect themselves.
   ③ Because they have changed their forms based on people's lifestyles.
   ④ Because they were considered clear and spotless.

2. What did the plague pandemic in the 14th century bring to the society? (Choose two options. The order does not matter.) ☐ ・ ☐
   ① Sewage systems　　　　　　② The Industrial Revolution
   ③ The Renaissance era　　　　④ The liberation of people

🔊 音の変化を理解して音読することができる。　　　　　　📖 人類と病気の戦いに関する英文を読んで，概要や要点を捉えることができる。
🔍 文脈を理解して適切な語句を用いて英文を完成することができる。　🎧 平易な英語で話される短い英文を聞いて必要な情報を聞き取ることができる。
💬 予防接種について簡単な語句を用いて考えを表現することができる。　✍ 医療について簡単な語句を用いて考えを表現することができる。

Goals

3. During the Industrial Revolution, workers fought against their employers as they
　　　　　.
　　① didn't have factories in rural areas
　　② had to work under bad working conditions
　　③ were hardly paid 　　　　　　　④ were not allowed to set up unions

🔍 Vocabulary & Grammar 　重要表現や文法事項について理解しよう【知識】　　英検® GTEC®

Make the correct choice to complete each sentence. (各2点)

1. Railway building increased (　　　) traffic needs in the city.
　　① for fear of 　　　② in response to 　　③ in spite of 　　④ on behalf of

2. Eating excessive amounts of apples every day may contribute to (　　　) issues.
　　① attractive 　　　② digestive 　　　③ effective 　　　④ sensitive

3. Red, black and green are used in the African (　　　) flag.
　　① acquisition 　　② devastation 　　③ liberation 　　④ reconsideration

4. I need to convince my (　　　) that I am worth more than I am being paid!
　　① employee 　　　② employer 　　　③ employment 　　④ unemployed

5. Drought, earthquakes and rats were (　　　) for unproductive years.
　　① beneficial 　　　② geographical 　　③ inevitable 　　④ responsible

🎧 Listening 　英文を聞いて理解しよう【知識・技能】【思考力・判断力・表現力】　　共通テスト 　CD 38

Listen to the English and make the best choice to match the content. (4点)

　① People could use drinking water in the mid-nineteenth century.
　② London developed one of the earliest sewage systems in the world.
　③ There were no sewage systems in London at the beginning of the 19th century.

💬 Interaction 　英文を聞いて会話を続けよう【知識・技能】【思考力・判断力・表現力】　スピーキング・トレーナー　CD 39

Listen to the English and respond to the last remark. (7点)

　［メ モ 　　　　　　　　　　　　　　　　　　　　　　　　　　　　　　　　　　　　　]

　アドバイス 　flu shot「インフルエンザ予防接種」

✏ Production (Write) 　自分の考えを書いて伝えよう【思考力・判断力・表現力】

Write your answer to the following question. (7点)

　Do you think future medical advancements will remove infectious diseases from the earth?

　アドバイス 　どちらを選ぶにしても，相手を納得させられるような理由を考えよう。

7 Thanks to the work / of many researchers and **physicians**, / we now have ways / to fight against infectious diseases. // One is **vaccination**. // By being **injected** / with a weaker form of the virus / before **contracting** the real one, / people can increase **immunity** / against the disease / it causes. // The French **chemist** / Louis Pasteur / developed this technique / for preventing **rabies** / in 1881. //

8 Another method is / taking **medication**, / which can kill or **weaken** / the virus or bacteria / in the body. // For example, / in 1928, / **penicillin** was discovered / by Alexander Fleming, / a **Scottish** physician-scientist. // It is a type of **antibiotic**, / which prevents the growth / of bacteria / or kills them. //

9 **Adjusting** our ways of life / to the **circumstances** / in which a disease occurs / may be another solution. // In the 19th century, / people finally discovered / that the cause of plague / was their unclean **sanitary** conditions. // They constructed a sewage system / and began / to use it. // This story may remind you / of the WHO's **declaration** / of a pandemic / in 2020, / which caused our lifestyles / to change. // Like the people of the past, / you may find it hard / to change your habits, / but getting used to a new lifestyle / and finding its beneficial aspects / may be the key / to living happy / and healthy lives. // (204 words)

🔊 **音読しよう**　　　　　　　　　　　　　　　　　スピーキング・トレーナー
Practice 1　スラッシュ位置で文を区切って読んでみよう ☐
Practice 2　音の変化に注意して読んでみよう ☐
TRY!　　　2分以内に本文全体を音読しよう ☐

📖 **Reading**　本文の内容を読んで理解しよう【知識・技能】【思考力・判断力・表現力】　　共通テスト

Make the correct choice to complete each sentence or answer each question. (各4点)

1. Which of the following is **not** true about vaccination? ☐
   ① It can kill or weaken the virus or bacteria.
   ② People can increase immunity against the disease by being injected with a weaker form of the virus.
   ③ The first one developed in 1881 was for rabies.
   ④ The French chemist Louis Pasteur developed the technique.

2. Penicillin ☐ .
   ① lives in human bodies
   ② prevents the growth of bacteria or kills them
   ③ was discovered as the cause of plague
   ④ was discovered by Alexander Fleming in 1881

3. Which of the following is **not** mentioned in the paragraphs as a means to fight against infectious diseases? ☐

　① Adjusting our ways of life to the circumstances　　② Lockdown
　③ Taking medication　　　　　　　　　　　　　　　④ Vaccination

🔍 Vocabulary & Grammar　重要表現や文法事項について理解しよう【知識】　英検® GTEC®

Make the correct choice to complete each sentence. (各2点)

1. (　　　) your seat belt properly before driving.
　① Adapt　　　　　② Adjust　　　　　③ Arrange　　　　④ Attach

2. Some medications can also (　　　) stomach microbes.
　① abolish　　　　② emit　　　　　③ survive　　　　④ weaken

3. The virus spreads more easily in areas with poor (　　　) conditions.
　① emergent　　　② ordinary　　　③ sanitary　　　④ toxic

4. The prom was the perfect (　　　) for Rei to wear her new dress.
　① accident　　　② circumstance　　③ intention　　④ residence

5. My youngest daughter is getting used (　　　) alone in her room.
　① sleep　　　　　② sleeping　　　　③ to sleep　　　　④ to sleeping

🎧 Listening　英文を聞いて理解しよう【知識・技能】【思考力・判断力・表現力】　共通テスト　CD 40

Listen to the English and make the best choice to match the content. (4点)

　① The listener doesn't seem to be in very good health.
　② The speaker has a cold.
　③ This statement was made in a very cold environment.

💬 Interaction　英文を聞いて会話を続けよう【知識・技能】【思考力・判断力・表現力】　スピーキング・トレーナー　CD 41

Listen to the English and respond to the last remark. (7点)

　〔メモ　　　　　　　　　　　　　　　　　　　　　　　　　　　　　　　〕

　アドバイス　知っていても知らなくても，Yes か No だけで終わらないようにしよう。

✏️ Production (Write)　自分の考えを書いて伝えよう【思考力・判断力・表現力】

Write your answer to the following question. (7点)

　Write your new habit that you started due to the COVID-19 pandemic and are still doing.

　アドバイス　habit「習慣」。感染拡大時に自分の習慣となった行動があるかどうか，考えてみよう。

You are studying / about the history / of infectious diseases. // You found the story / of Louis Pasteur. //

In the 1880s, / rabies met its match / in a French scientist / named Louis Pasteur. // In 1881, / all Pasteur knew for certain / was that the disease was carried / to humans / in the **saliva** / of **rabid** animals. // He figured / that the **germ** had to travel / from the bite / to the victim's brain / and **spinal** cord. // After identifying the germ, / he was able to develop a **vaccine**. // Finally, / he proved / it was effective / on an animal / attacked by a rabid animal. //

But would the vaccine also prove effective / on humans? // Pasteur was **reluctant** / to try it. // What if Pasteur injected a person / with the rabies vaccine / and gave him the disease / instead of **curing** him? // There was only one thing for him to do: / test the vaccine / on himself. //

As Pasteur made preparations / for this **drastic** step, / a nine-year-old boy / named Joseph / and his mother came / to his office. // The boy had just been **viciously** attacked / by a rabid dog / on his way to school. // But his mother was focused / not on his **wounds** / but on the possibility / of rabies. //

Pasteur pointed out / the **grave** risks involved. // But the mother **pleaded** with Pasteur / to save him. // Since Pasteur wasn't a medical doctor, / he had to ask doctors / to examine Joseph's wounds. // They **urged** Pasteur / to use his vaccine. // Pasteur decided to take the risk. //

On the first day, / Pasteur injected Joseph / with a very **mild** form / of the germ. // Each day, / he gave the boy / a **slightly** stronger **dose**. // On the 14th day, / Pasteur injected Joseph / with a very powerful dose. // Joseph, / however, / showed no signs / of the disease. //

Still, / Pasteur had to wait and watch. // Perhaps / the rabies was just taking its time / to reach the boy's spinal cord / and brain. // But as each day passed / with no sign of disease, / Pasteur's hopes rose. // Joseph might live! // Not only would that be a personal victory / for Pasteur and the boy, / but it would signal / that the disease was finally conquered. // In August, / Pasteur was finally convinced. // "It has been 31 days / since Joseph was bitten," / he wrote / in his notebook. // "He is now quite safe. // The vaccine is successful." // (357 words)

🔊 音読しよう　　　　　　　　　　　　　　　　　　　スピーキング・トレーナー

Practice 1　スラッシュ位置で文を区切って読んでみよう ☐
Practice 2　音の変化に注意して読んでみよう ☐
TRY!　　　　3分30秒以内に本文全体を音読しよう ☐

Goals

◀️ 音の変化を理解して音読することができる。　　　　　　　📖 パスツールに関する英文を読んで，概要や要点を捉えることができる。
🔍 文脈を理解して適切な語句を用いて英文を完成することができる。
🎧 やや長めの英文を聞いて必要な情報を聞き取ることができる。

📖 Reading　本文の内容を読んで理解しよう【知識・技能】【思考力・判断力・表現力】　共通テスト

Make the correct choice to answer each question. (各6点)

1. What does "reluctant" mean in line 10? ☐

① enthusiastic　　② modest　　③ unwilling　　④ weird

2. Put the events in the order they occurred. ☐ → ☐ → ☐ → ☐ → ☐

① A nine-year-old boy named Joseph and his mother came to his office.

② Pasteur developed a vaccine and proved it was effective on an animal.

③ Pasteur identified the germ of rabies.

④ Pasteur injected Joseph with a very mild form of the germ.

⑤ Pasteur injected Joseph with a very powerful dose.

🔍 Vocabulary & Grammar　重要表現や文法事項について理解しよう【知識】　英検® GTEC®

Make the correct choice to complete each sentence. (各2点)

1. My doctor strongly (　　　) me to give up smoking.

① avoided　　② forced　　③ tortured　　④ urged

2. We need to take (　　　) steps globally to reduce CO_2 emissions.

① alternative　　② drastic　　③ opposite　　④ physical

3. Sleeping is the best (　　　) for your fatigue.

① aid　　② cure　　③ plan　　④ strategy

4. The boy (　　　) with his mom not to leave him alone in the bedroom.

① begged　　② dealt　　③ pleaded　　④ reacted

5. (　　　) collapsed on the hotel bed than she fell asleep.

① Never had she　② No sooner had she　③ Not only had she　④ Not until had she

🎧 Listening　英文を聞いて理解しよう【知識・技能】【思考力・判断力・表現力】　共通テスト　CD 42

Listen to the English and make the best choice to match the content. (各6点)

1. Where were four Japanese infected by rabies?

① All in India.　　　　　　　　② All in Japan.

③ Both inside and outside Japan.　④ Somewhere outside of Japan.

2. According to the speaker, what is true about the situation in India?

① Around two thousand people die of rabies every year.

② Most dogs suffering from rabies are killed.

③ People are against killing wild dogs.

④ Some people live with dogs for religious reasons.

3. How long does it take to finish all the rabies vaccinations in Japan?

① In three or four days.　　② In two weeks.

③ In three to four weeks.　　④ In three months.

Eating well / is an essential part of athletes' training / which has gained attention / recently. // Let's learn about sports nutrition. //

① During the New Year season, / many people watch the Tokyo-Hakone **Collegiate** "Ekiden" Road **Relay**. // Teams of university students leave Tokyo, / running to Hakone and back / over two days. // Each team member covers a **segment** / of the total distance. // As Hakone is a mountainous area / and the round-trip distance is a long 217.9 kilometers, / this popular race is regarded / as one of the most challenging races / in Japan. //

② In 2012, / Toyo University won first prize, / setting a race record. // It was true / that all members of the team / were **competent** runners, / but they also had a secret weapon / that supported their efforts: / Professor Kazuhiro Uenishi / and his students / at Kagawa Nutrition University. // They analyzed each runner's **nutritional** condition / by examining their blood / and measuring their body-fat **percentage** / and bone **density**. // They also developed a meal menu / for each runner / to build a fit and strong body. // During a few days / just before the race, / they made meals / for the team. //

③ Professor Uenishi has been giving some **guidance** / on nutrition / to other teams and athletes / in a variety of sports. // There are some points / athletes should keep in mind / **concerning** what and how they eat. // Let's take a look at each point. // (200 words)

🔊 **音読しよう**

スピーキング・トレーナー

Practice 1 スラッシュ位置で文を区切って読んでみよう □
Practice 2 音の変化に注意して読んでみよう □
TRY ! 2分以内に本文全体を音読しよう □

📖 **Reading** 本文の内容を読んで理解しよう【知識・技能】【思考力・判断力・表現力】 共通テスト

Make the correct choice to complete each sentence or answer each question. (各4点)

1. Which of the following is **not** true about the Tokyo-Hakone Collegiate "Ekiden" Road Relay? ☐

   ① It is popular and many people watch it during the New Year season.
   ② It is said that it's one of the most challenging races in Japan.
   ③ Teams of university students run over two days and two nights.
   ④ The total distance of the round-trip is a 217.9 kilometers.

2. The ': (colon)' in line 11 is used to ☐ .

   ① add explanation to the previous sentence ② emphasize the previous sentence
   ③ link to an independent clause ④ show an example

3. What is the main subject of Professor Uenishi's guidance? ☐

① Athlete performance　　　　② Exercise routines

③ Nutrition　　　　　　　　　④ Sports equipment

🔍 Vocabulary & Grammar　重要表現や文法事項について理解しよう【知識】　英検® GTEC®

Make the correct choice to complete each sentence. (各2点)

1. Everyone in the town has (　　　) him as a leader.

① attended　　　② observed　　　③ regarded　　　④ spied

2. Before reading the textbook, Rick (　　　) a quick look at the table of contents.

① caught　　　② held　　　③ took　　　④ viewed

3. The subway system allows the city with few traffic problems despite the high population (　　　).

① concentration　　② density　　③ tightness　　④ zone

4. Nobody can become a (　　　) pianist without practice.

① competent　　② justified　　③ proper　　④ strict

5. (　　　) for her son, she made some tea.

① By waiting　　② Not waited　　③ Waited　　④ Waiting

🎧 Listening　英文を聞いて理解しよう【知識・技能】【思考力・判断力・表現力】　共通テスト CD 43

Listen to the English and make the best choice to match the content. (4点)

① The Ekiden race was competed by eight teams.

② The speaker finished his student life as a runner.

③ The university team ranked eighth in the Ekiden race.

💬 Interaction　英文を聞いて会話を続けよう【知識・技能】【思考力・判断力・表現力】　スピーキング・トレーナー　CD 44

Listen to the English and respond to the last remark. (7点)

［メモ　　　　　　　　　　　　　　　　　　　　　　　　　　　　　　　　　］

アドバイス　相手の発言のように具体的に何をしているかを答えよう。

💬 Production (Speak)　自分の考えを話して伝えよう【思考力・判断力・表現力】　スピーキング・トレーナー

Speak out your answer to the following question. (7点)

Besides having proper meals and practices, what else do you think is needed for competent athletes?

アドバイス　「精神的強さ」や「チームワーク」など食事と練習以外のことを答え，そう思う理由などを付け加えよう。

④ First, / it's important / to eat three meals / a day. // If you **skip** breakfast, / your body will suffer / from lack of nutrition. // If you skip dinner, / your **muscles** will not be repaired / and get weaker. // Sugar quickly changes / to an energy source / for your brain and muscles. // It is contained / in **staple** foods / such as rice, / bread / or pasta. // Eating three meals a day / is the basis of a healthy diet. //

⑤ Second, / you should add / main and side dishes, / fruits / and **dairy** products / to the staple food. // The main dish should be one / like steak / or baked fish, / and the side dish should be salad / or vegetables. // In this way, / you can take in / almost all of the **nutrients** / your body needs. // When you want to eat pasta dishes / or pizza, / adding side dishes and dairy products / will make your meal / healthier. //

⑥ Third, / for people who play sports, / it's essential / to **supplement** nutrition / by eating between meals. // Athletes often use up / lots of energy / and need sugar. // You may think of high-energy foods / such as potato **chips** / and chocolate, / but rice balls / and fruits / might be better alternatives. // (187 words)

🔊 **音読しよう**　　　　　　　　　　　　　スピーキング・トレーナー

Practice 1　スラッシュ位置で文を区切って読んでみよう☐
Practice 2　音の変化に注意して読んでみよう☐
TRY！　　　1分50秒以内に本文全体を音読しよう☐

📖 **Reading**　本文の内容を読んで理解しよう【知識・技能】【思考力・判断力・表現力】　　共通テスト

Make the correct choice to complete each sentence or answer each question. (各4点)

1. Sugar is important for your body as ☐ .

① it is the basis of a healthy diet

② it quickly changes to an energy source for your brain and muscles

③ your body will suffer when lacking of it

④ your muscles will not be repaired and get weaker without it

2. You are going to eat grilled fish as your main dish. Which of the following is an appropriate addition as a side dish? ☐

① chocolate　　　② pasta　　　③ steak　　　④ vegetable soup

3. Which of the following is true about sports nutrition? ☐

① Athletes often use up lots of energy and need sugar.

② High-energy foods such as potato chips and chocolate are ideal for athletes.

③ It's essential to avoid eating between meals.

④ Rice balls and fruits are good for athletes' staple foods.

🔎 Vocabulary & Grammar　重要表現や文法事項について理解しよう【知識】　英検® GTEC®

Make the correct choice to complete each sentence. (各2点)

1. Meg used (　　　) almost all the money she had saved to buy the latest smartphone.
   ① in　　　　　② out　　　　　③ up　　　　　④ with

2. Giant pandas' (　　　) food is bamboo.
   ① majority　　　② nature　　　③ staple　　　④ whole

3. I think I just (　　　) a line. I lost track of how far I had read.
   ① drew　　　　② found　　　　③ skipped　　　④ shot

4. Vegetarians may need to (　　　) their diet with iron.
   ① add　　　　② imply　　　③ supplement　　　④ supply

5. Only one minute delay (　　　) her miss the bus.
   ① caused　　　② led　　　③ let　　　④ made

🎧 Listening　英文を聞いて理解しよう【知識・技能】【思考力・判断力・表現力】　共通テスト CD 45

Listen to the English and make the best choice to match the content. (4点)

① Roast pork is less popular than fish fry.

② The listener is likely to have fish for lunch.

③ The speaker won't eat the pork lunch set.

💬 Interaction　英文を聞いて会話を続けよう【知識・技能】【思考力・判断力・表現力】　スピーキング・トレーナー CD 46

Listen to the English and respond to the last remark. (7点)

[メモ　　　　　　　　　　　　　　　　　　　　　　　　　　　　　　　　　　　　　　]

アドバイス　理由や補足情報を付け加えよう。質問に答えた後に，相手にアドバイスをしてもよい。

✐ Production (Write)　自分の考えを書いて伝えよう【思考力・判断力・表現力】

Write your answer to the following question. (7点)

How often do you eat high-energy foods such as potato chips or chocolate?

アドバイス　頻度を答えるだけでなく，自分がそれをどう思っているか表現しよう。

----

7 It is also important / to choose foods / for sports nutrition / depending on the **intended** purpose. // In order to **strengthen** muscles, / athletes should take in / one to two **grams** of protein / per kilogram of their body weight. // Beef, / chicken, / and fish / such as **tuna** and **bonito** / contain lots of protein. // Sugar is also important / for muscles. // If our body runs short / of sugar, / it will **extract** energy / from protein / instead. // That will result in weakened muscles. //

8 For strengthening bones / in order to prevent injuries, / athletes need **plenty** of **calcium**. // Calcium tends to be lost / through **sweating**, / but **vitamin** K helps bones / take it in. // Vitamin D also encourages our body / to **absorb** calcium / and **deactivates** so-called bone-destroying cells. // Calcium is found / in milk / and other dairy products. // Vitamin K is **plentiful** / in *natto* / and green-leaf vegetables. // Mushrooms and fish / such as **sardines** / are excellent sources / of vitamin D. //

9 When Professor Uenishi's students graduated / from university, / they said, / "By **managing** the nutritional states / of runners, / we gained a sense / of responsibility / for supplying nutritious meals. // Food is the basis / of human life." // Human bodies are made / from what we eat. // Proper daily meals are sure / to make your body / strong and healthy. // (200 words)

🔊 **音読しよう**　　　　　　　　　　　　　　　スピーキング・トレーナー
Practice 1　スラッシュ位置で文を区切って読んでみよう □
Practice 2　音の変化に注意して読んでみよう □
TRY！　　　2分以内に本文全体を音読しよう □

📖 **Reading**　本文の内容を読んで理解しよう【知識・技能】【思考力・判断力・表現力】　共通テスト

Make the correct choice to complete each sentence or answer each question. (各4点)

1. What does the author claim about sugar in paragraph 7? ⬚
   ① Beef, chicken, tuna and bonito contain a lot of it.
   ② It is not beneficial for athletes.
   ③ Lack of it may cause weakened muscles.
   ④ Consuming it as much as possible will strengthen muscles.

2. Which of the following is **not** true? ⬚
   ① Mushrooms and fish such as sardines are excellent sources of calcium.
   ② Plenty of calcium is essential for athletes.
   ③ Vitamin D helps absorb calcium and deactivates bone-destroying cells.
   ④ Vitamin K, which is plentiful in *natto* and green-leaf vegetables, helps bones take calcium in.

3. One **opinion** about sports nutrition is that ☐ .

　① beef, chicken, and fish contain protein

　② calcium is found in milk

　③ calcium tends to be lost through sweating

　④ food is the basis of human life

🔍 **Vocabulary & Grammar**　重要表現や文法事項について理解しよう【知識】　　　　　英検® GTEC®

Make the correct choice to complete each sentence.（各2点）

1. Don't give up. You can still make (　　　　) of progress.

　① bit　　　　　② excess　　　　　③ plenty　　　　　④ surplus

2. Foods such as meat and dairy products have begun to (　　　　) short.

　① be　　　　　② come　　　　　③ fall　　　　　④ run

3. We need to (　　　　) the proper use of the meeting room.

　① afford　　　　② cope　　　　　③ decline　　　　④ manage

4. Having run around the playground, the children were all covered in (　　　　).

　① insight　　　　② livestock　　　③ sweat　　　　④ tear

5. My grandmother likes (　　　　) French food and Italian food.

　① both　　　　　② either　　　　　③ neither　　　　④ whichever

🎧 **Listening**　英文を聞いて理解しよう【知識・技能】【思考力・判断力・表現力】　　共通テスト　CD 47

Listen to the English and make the best choice to match the content.（4点）

　① Kaori has been studying for a long time to become a specialist.

　② Kaori is looking for someone who knows well about nutrition.

　③ The speaker won't work with Kaori next summer.

💬 **Interaction**　英文を聞いて会話を続けよう【知識・技能】【思考力・判断力・表現力】　スピーキング・トレーナー　CD 48

Listen to the English and respond to the last remark.（7点）

　[メモ　　　　　　　　　　　　　　　　　　　　　　　　　　　　　　　　　　]

　アドバイス　相手の発言と質問から，何に困っているかを解釈しよう。

✐ **Production（Write）**　自分の考えを書いて伝えよう【思考力・判断力・表現力】

Write your answer to the following question.（7点）

　Do you cook?

　アドバイス　短い質問だが，話題を広げて自分のことについて表現しよう。

You're starting to think / about improving your eating habits. // You have found / some recipes / on the Internet. //

Chicken liver in cream //

Ingredients (for 2 people) //

Chicken livers: / 200 g // Salt: / 1 g // **Pepper**: / one **pinch** // Onion: / 1/2 // *Maitake*: / 100 g // Butter: / 8 g // **Sliced garlic**: / 1/2 // **Flour**: / two tsp // White **wine**: / one tbsp // Milk: / 3/4 cup // Fresh cream: / 1/4 cup //

Nutrition information / (per person) //

- Energy: / 324 kcal // ● Fat: / 18.6 g // **Carbohydrate**: / 14.7 g //
- Protein: / 23.9 g // ● Vitamin B6: / 0.81 mg //

How to cook //

1. Cut the chicken livers / into bite-sized pieces / and place them / in salt water. // Then, / get rid of all the **moisture** / off the chicken liver pieces / and add the salt and pepper to them. //
2. Cut an onion / along the fibers / and then / into pieces one centimeter wide. // Break up a *maitake* mushroom / into pieces. //
3. Put some butter, / some slices of garlic / and the chicken liver pieces / into a **frying pan**, / and cook both sides of the liver / on medium heat. //
4. Add the slices of the onion, / the pieces of *maitake* mushroom / and flour, / and fry them / until the flour completely disappears. //
5. Add a small amount of white wine / over everything. // Then, add milk and fresh cream / when the **liquid** is gone. // Finally, / **boil** on medium heat / until the **sauce thickens**, / and finish with some salt and pepper. //

Salmon and spinach gratin //

Ingredients / (for 2 people) //

Salmon: / 200 g // Salt: / 2 g // Onion: / 80 g // Spinach: / 150 g // Butter: / 12 g // *Sake*: / two tbsp // Water: / two tbsp // Milk: / 1/4 cup // **Ketchup**: / one tbsp // Cheese: / 30 g //

Nutrition information / (per person) //

- Energy: / 294 kcal // ● Fat: / 12.8 g // ● Carbohydrate: / 10.8 g //
- Calcium: / 235 mg // ● Vitamin D: / 32.2 μg // ● Vitamin K: / 170 μg //

How to cook //

1. Remove the skin / from the salmon, / cut it / into four pieces, / and add some salt and pepper / on top. //
2. Cut the onion / into slices. // Boil the spinach, / remove the excess moisture / and cut it / into pieces / four or five centimeters long. //
3. Fry the onion slices / for one or two minutes / with some butter / in a frying pan. // Add the salmon, / *sake* / and water. // Cover and fry the salmon / on low heat / for two or three minutes, / then / take the salmon / out of the frying pan. //
4. Add spinach, / milk / and ketchup / to the pan, / and mix them / with 20 grams of the cheese. // Move all the ingredients / from the frying pan / to a dish, / and add the salmon / and the remaining 10 grams of cheese / to them. // Finally, / bake everything / in an **oven** / for six to seven minutes / until the cheese is browned. // (433 words)

◀)) **音読しよう**　　　　　　　　　　　　　　　　　スピーキング・トレーナー

Practice 1　スラッシュ位置で文を区切って読んでみよう ☐

Practice 2　音の変化に注意して読んでみよう ☐

TRY！　　　４分50秒以内に本文全体を音読しよう ☐

📖 **Reading**　本文の内容を読んで理解しよう【知識・技能】【思考力・判断力・表現力】　共通テスト

Make the correct choice to complete the sentence below. (完答12点)

1. According to the recipe and Lesson 7 as a whole, ☐A☐ strengthens our bones because ☐B☐.

　☐A☐ : ① Chicken liver in cream　　② Salmon and spinach gratin

　☐B☐ : ① it includes much protein　　② it provides you more carbohydrate

　　　　③ it has less energy and fat　　④ it includes milk, cheese, Vitamin D and K

🔍 **Vocabulary & Grammar**　重要表現や文法事項について理解しよう【知識】　英検® GTEC®

Make the correct choice to complete each sentence. (各4点)

1. My grandmother likes red wine (　　　　) with orange juice.

　① combined　　　② divided　　　③ mixed　　　④ turned

2. Rice is a main (　　　) in Arab cuisine.

　① aspect　　　② component　　　③ ingredient　　　④ nutrition

3. COVID-19 raised the demand for staple food such as pasta and (　　　).

　① beer　　　② flour　　　③ milk　　　④ salads

4. The sensors always monitor (　　　) levels in the soil.

　① humidity　　　② mist　　　③ moisture　　　④ wetness

🎧 **Listening**　英文を聞いて理解しよう【知識・技能】【思考力・判断力・表現力】　共通テスト　CD 49

Listen to the English and make the best choice to match the content. (各4点)

1. Which part of the chicken does the speaker use?

　① Breasts　　　② Legs　　　③ Livers　　　④ Wings

2. What do we have to do before we cut chicken?

　① Cool in a refrigerator　　　② Make holes with a fork

　③ Press with a hammer　　　④ Remove its skin

3. Which of the following is true about the process of cooking?

　① We bake the chicken in an oven.

　② We cook with high and then with low heat.

　③ We have to cool the chicken for about an hour.

　④ We need some eggs to season the chicken.

"I want to cross over rivers / and the sea." // With such a hope / in mind, / people have built / a wide variety of bridges. // Do you know / how they are built? // What kinds of science are hidden / in them? //

① The history of bridges is human history. // Since ancient times, / human beings have **flourished** / around water. // They imagined / how crossing over bodies of water / would make travel / much faster. // The first bridges were simple; / they were made from things / like fallen trees, / making it faster and easier / to connect two places. // Although stronger materials / such as stone came to be used / in bridge construction, / there were still limitations / on bridge **length**. // These limitations led / to new developments. //

② One example is the stone **arch** bridge, / used by the **Romans** / to build the first large, / strong bridges. // This type of bridge / depended on **gravity** / holding **wedge**-shaped stones together. // Since the stones weighed so much, / the friction between them / was huge / and they wouldn't slide apart. //

③ Another development / was the **suspension** bridge. // It was originally made / by combining several **vines** / and **suspending** them / from one point to another. // The first suspension bridges were designed / with the **walkway** of the bridge / supported by two lines that were fixed / at both ends. // They had no towers or **piers**. // The lines, / which followed a **shallow downward arc**, / moved in response to **loads** / on the bridge. // (189 words)

◆) 音読しよう　　　　　　　　　　　　　　　　スピーキング・トレーナー

Practice 1　スラッシュ位置で文を区切って読んでみよう □
Practice 2　音の変化に注意して読んでみよう □
TRY！　　　１分50秒以内に本文全体を音読しよう □

📖 **Reading**　本文の内容を読んで理解しよう【知識・技能】【思考力・判断力・表現力】　　　共通テスト

Make the correct choice to complete each sentence or answer each question. (各4点)

1. What does "flourished" mean in line 5? _____
   ① avoided　　　② bloomed　　　③ fought　　　④ gathered

2. Which of the following is **not** true about the first stone arch bridge? _____
   ① It depended on gravity holding wedge-shaped stones together.
   ② It was first used by the Greeks.
   ③ Since the stones weighed so much, the friction between them was huge.
   ④ The stones wouldn't slide apart due to the huge friction.

- 音の変化を理解して音読することができる。
- 文脈を理解して適切な語句を用いて英文を完成することができる。
- つり橋について簡単な語句を用いて考えを表現することができる。
- 橋の歴史に関する英文を読んで概要や要点を捉えることができる。
- 平易な英語で話される短い英文を聞いて必要な情報を聞き取ることができる。
- 古代に作られたものについて簡単な語句を用いて説明することができる。

Goals

3. The first suspension bridge was ☐.

  ① another development but it soon fell out of use

  ② made of plants   ③ suspended from towers or piers

  ④ too firm to move in response to loads on the bridge

🔍 **Vocabulary & Grammar**   重要表現や文法事項について理解しよう【知識】   英検® GTEC®

Make the correct choice to complete each sentence. (各2点)

1. The town of Sakai continued to (   ) under the rule of Oda Nobunaga.

  ① amuse   ② flourish   ③ improve   ④ struggle

2. Japan possesses large ocean territories with a combination of various depths from
(   ) to deep sea.

  ① awkward   ② broad   ③ narrow   ④ shallow

3. The center divider is used to prevent vehicles from (   ) over it and striking
an oncoming vehicle.

  ① crossing   ② leaning   ③ looking   ④ taking

4. The truck carrying the heavy (   ) gradually slowed down.

  ① load   ② loud   ③ lord   ④ road

5. The girls remained (   ) on the beach.

  ① laid   ② laying   ③ lying   ④ to lie

🎧 **Listening**   英文を聞いて理解しよう【知識・技能】【思考力・判断力・表現力】   共通テスト CD 50

Listen to the English and make the best choice to match the content. (4点)

  ① The speaker is crossing the suspension bridge.

  ② The suspension bridge is the longest in Asia.

  ③ There is another higher suspension bridge in Asia.

💬 **Interaction**   英文を聞いて会話を続けよう【知識・技能】【思考力・判断力・表現力】   スピーキング・トレーナー CD 51

Listen to the English and respond to the last remark. (7点)

[メモ   ]

アドバイス ない場合は，渡ってみたいかどうかを表現しよう。

💬 **Production（Speak）**   自分の考えを話して伝えよう【思考力・判断力・表現力】   スピーキング・トレーナー

Speak out your answer to the following question. (7点)

We have learned that the history of the bridge goes back to ancient times. What
else can you think of that humans have used since ancient times?

アドバイス 思いつかなければ，スマートフォンなどを使って調べてみよう。

④ The structures of bridges differ / depending on their length / and purpose. // The main **components** of a bridge / are the foundation, / the **substructure**, / and the **superstructure**. // Each of them consists of important parts, / and the superstructure determines / the form of the bridge. // The three basic bridge forms are / the beam, / the suspension / and the **truss**. //

⑤ Beam bridges are / the most common type of bridge. // A beam carries **vertical** loads / by bending. // Its structure is rather simple / and appropriate / for short bridges. // Suspension bridges, / which can cover long **spans**, / carry vertical loads / through **tension** in lines. // The load is **transferred** / both to the towers and to the **anchorages**, / which withstand the **inward** and vertical pull / of the **cables**. //

⑥ Truss bridges are used / to support great weight. // They are suitable / for **railroad** and covered bridges. // The amount of material / needed to construct them / is small / compared to the weight / they can support. // A truss is a combination / of many triangles / which makes a stable form, / **capable** of supporting a **considerable external** load / over a large span. // The triangle reduces the stress / caused by any force. // If a corner of any triangle has a force / on it, / the two sides which make that corner / **squeeze** together, / and the third side **stretches**. // In this way, / triangles divide any force / placed on them. //

(217 words)

🔊 音読しよう   スピーキング・トレーナー
Practice 1　スラッシュ位置で文を区切って読んでみよう □
Practice 2　音の変化に注意して読んでみよう □
TRY！　　　2分10秒以内に本文全体を音読しよう □

📖 **Reading**　本文の内容を読んで理解しよう【知識・技能】【思考力・判断力・表現力】　　共通テスト

Make the correct choice to answer each question. (各4点)

1. According to paragraph 4, what determines the structures of bridges? ⬚
   ① The beam, the suspension and the truss.　　② The design and cost.
   ③ The foundation, the substructure, and the superstructure.
   ④ The length and purpose.

2. Choose the characteristics of beam bridges and suspension bridges. (Choose two options for each. The order does not matter.)
   Beam bridges ⬚ · ⬚　　　　　Suspension bridges ⬚ · ⬚
   ① Appropriate for long bridges　　② Appropriate for short bridges
   ③ Bends to withstand vertical loads　④ Good for railroad and covered bridges
   ⑤ The towers and the anchorages support the load transmitted to the main cable.

3. Which of the following bridge is most suitable for heavy weight? ☐
　① Arch bridge　　② Beam bridge　　③ Suspension bridge　　④ Truss bridge

🔍 **Vocabulary & Grammar**　重要表現や文法事項について理解しよう【知識】　英検® GTEC®

Make the correct choice to complete each sentence. (各2点)

1. Do you think this black dress is (　　) for my friend's wedding?
　① adequate　　② capable　　③ match　　④ suitable

2. Protein is another key (　　) of a healthy, balanced diet.
　① component　　② member　　③ portion　　④ supply

3. The kitten looked truly tiny (　　) the panda.
　① compared to　　② judging from　　③ relative to　　④ speaking of

4. The Titanic rose to a nearly (　　) angle before it sank.
　① flat　　② horizontal　　③ oval　　④ vertical

5. (　　), she will achieve great success as a musician.
　① Be talented　　② Been talented　　③ Having talented　　④ Talented

🎧 **Listening**　英文を聞いて理解しよう【知識・技能】【思考力・判断力・表現力】　共通テスト　CD 52

Listen to the English and make the best choice to match the content. (4点)
　① The expressway has twelve bridges in total.
　② The number of beam bridges is larger than that of truss bridges.
　③ You can cross the river with the expressway.

💬 **Interaction**　英文を聞いて会話を続けよう【知識・技能】【思考力・判断力・表現力】　スピーキング・トレーナー　CD 53

Listen to the English and respond to the last remark. (7点)
　[メモ　　　　　　　　　　　　　　　　　　　　　　　　　　　　　　　　　　]
　アドバイス　有名ではなくても、興味があって描写できるものなら何を挙げてもよい。

✏️ **Production (Write)**　自分の考えを書いて伝えよう【思考力・判断力・表現力】

Write your answer to the following question. (7点)
　Write your unforgettable memory related to bridges.
　アドバイス　橋に関連していれば何でもよいので、描写してみよう。

⑦ When people choose / which type of bridge to build, / they make decisions / based on the **requirements**: / the weight of expected traffic, / the environment of the area / and other factors. // Bridges are **critical** parts / of society's infrastructure. // Their purpose is / to help people move around safely, / so their **structural** designs need to be safe. //

⑧ **Additionally**, / bridges have an important role / to play / as local **landmarks** / in our society. // The Lucky **Knot** Bridge / in China / is one of many **stunning** landmark bridges. // The design was inspired / by the **Möbius strip**, / as well as the traditional **decorative** knot-tying / of Chinese folk art, / where the knot symbolizes / luck and **prosperity**. // The Tower Bridge is an attractive landmark / in London. // It is a huge suspension bridge / that spans the River Thames / and it is also a **raisable** bridge / which can let large ships through. // It is known / as an **iconic** symbol / of London. //

⑨ In these ways, / bridges are not only important infrastructures / for transportation, / but they also have interesting design aspects. // Bridges are useful, / and are also pieces of art / and history. // Bridges help us connect our communities / and bring us closer / together. // (188 words)

🔊 **音読しよう**　　　　　　　　　　　　　　　　　　　スピーキング・トレーナー

Practice 1　スラッシュ位置で文を区切って読んでみよう ☐
Practice 2　音の変化に注意して読んでみよう ☐
TRY！　　　１分40秒以内に本文全体を音読しよう ☐

📖 **Reading**　本文の内容を読んで理解しよう【知識・技能】【思考力・判断力・表現力】　　共通テスト

Make the correct choice to complete each sentence or answer each question. (各4点)

1. What does "critical" mean in line 3? ☐

　① analytical　　　② essential　　　③ material　　　④ surplus

2. The Lucky Knot Bridge ☐.

　① is a raisable bridge which can let large ships through

　② is an attractive landmark in London

　③ was built as a symbol of luck and prosperity

　④ was designed based on a Möbius strip as well as Chinese knotting

3. Which of the following is **not** true about bridges? ☐

　① They help people move around safely.

　② They are usually built to be local landmarks in our society.

　③ They are useful, and are also pieces of art and history.

　④ They are critical parts of society's infrastructure.

Goals
● 音の変化を理解して音読することができる。
📖 橋の役割に関する英文を読んで，概要や要点を捉えることができる。
🔍 文脈を理解して適切な語句を用いて英文を完成することができる。
🎧 平易な英語で話される短い英文を聞いて必要な情報を聞き取ることができる。
🗣 カレンダーについて簡単な語句を用いて説明することができる。
✎ 地元のランドマークについて簡単な語句を用いて説明することができる。

🔍 Vocabulary & Grammar   重要表現や文法事項について理解しよう【知識】   英検® GTEC®

Make the correct choice to complete each sentence. (各 2 点)

1. My smartphone does not meet the (   ) for the new game.
   ① advantages   ② conditions   ③ control   ④ requirements

2. Pull over and (   ) the emergency vehicles through!
   ① go   ② let   ③ put   ④ run

3. They got to the beach in time and saw a (   ) sunset.
   ① crucial   ② stunning   ③ typical   ④ virtual

4. The city of Rome has grown in population and (   ) over the centuries.
   ① efficiency   ② prosperity   ③ struggle   ④ virtue

5. (   ) by the news of the accident, my mother called me.
   ① Being worrying   ② To worry   ③ Worrying   ④ Worried

🎧 Listening   英文を聞いて理解しよう【知識・技能】【思考力・判断力・表現力】   共通テスト   CD 54

Listen to the English and make the best choice to match the content. (4 点)

   ① One of the towers of this bridge is made of stone.

   ② The speaker doesn't know this bridge very well.

   ③ Stone is not the only material used to build both towers.

💬 Interaction   英文を聞いて会話を続けよう【知識・技能】【思考力・判断力・表現力】   スピーキング・トレーナー   CD 55

Listen to the English and respond to the last remark. (7 点)

   〔メ モ   〕

   アドバイス 「今日は何の日」の例を一つ思い出そう。

✎ Production (Write)   自分の考えを書いて伝えよう【思考力・判断力・表現力】

Write your answer to the following question. (7 点)

   Describe the landmark in your hometown. Or name one you want to visit.

   アドバイス 観覧車や橋，特徴的な建物などを挙げてみよう。

Suppose / you are a construction worker / in your city. // Recently, / three bridges / in the city center / have gotten old. // The city wants to improve these bridges. // Listen to the request / from the city. //

Location A: / This area is a **residential** neighborhood / where **aesthetics** are important, / so high buildings are prohibited. // Although the span of the new bridge must cover / only 15 meters, / it should be finished / as soon as possible / because many tourists and local people / cross over the river / at this location. // It will be for **pedestrians** / only. // A simple structure with basic support / will be enough. //

Location B: / This bridge is the main hub / to connect to the city center. // The new bridge will be 300 meters long, / spanning the wide river. // We want it / to become another landmark / of this city. // This spot is expected / to have heavy traffic, / so the new bridge must be easy / to maintain. //

Location C: / This bridge is for **freight** trains / carrying **iron ore**. // Due to the **extreme** heat / last month, / some parts were damaged. // The new bridge should be strong enough / to **endure** both heavy loads / and extreme weather conditions. // It will be 150 meters long. //
(162words)

🔊 **音読しよう**

スピーキング・トレーナー

Practice 1　スラッシュ位置で文を区切って読んでみよう ☐
Practice 2　音の変化に注意して読んでみよう ☐
TRY !　　　1分40秒以内に本文全体を音読しよう ☐

📖 **Reading**　本文の内容を読んで理解しよう【知識・技能】【思考力・判断力・表現力】　　共通テスト

Make the correct choice to complete each sentence or answer each question.

1. Which of the following is **not** true about Location A? ☐ 　(1., 3.：各4点, 2.：6点)

　① It is in a residential neighborhood where aesthetics are important.

　② It is necessary for the bridge to cover 150 meters.

　③ High buildings are prohibited.

　④ Many tourists and local people cross over the river.

2. Which type of bridge is most likely the best choice for location B?　Choose the correct answer based on the whole Lesson 8 story. ☐

　① Arch bridge　　　　　　　② Beam bridge
　③ Suspension bridge　　　　④ Truss bridge

3. The bridge for Location C ⬚.

　① is currently damaged

　② is expected to be a new landmark of the city

　③ is in a touristic place where many pedestrians cross

　④ will be the longest one of the three bridges

🔍 Vocabulary & Grammar　重要表現や文法事項について理解しよう【知識】　　英検® GTEC®

Make the correct choice to complete each sentence. (各2点)

1. I was (　　　) to be on a flight to Hawaii if this big typhoon didn't hit us.

　① already　　　　② managed　　　　③ required　　　　④ supposed

2. There is an undersea (　　　) tunnel between Shimonoseki and Kita Kyushu.

　① passenger　　　② pedestrian　　　③ running　　　　④ walking

3. The rocket flew to the moon at (　　　) speeds.

　① average　　　　② extreme　　　　③ ordinary　　　　④ supreme

4. How did you (　　　) the customer's rudeness?

　① endure　　　　② survive　　　　③ remain　　　　④ withdraw

5. The calm town is a (　　　) suburb of Nagoya.

　① commercial　　　② potential　　　③ presidential　　　④ residential

6. Will you pick me up tomorrow? I'm sending you the (　　　) of my apartment.

　① acquisition　　　② destination　　　③ location　　　　④ prescription

7. The large object from space hit the area, (　　　) the building.

　① destroyed　　　② destroying　　　③ and destroy　　　④ to destroy

🎧 Listening　英文を聞いて理解しよう【知識・技能】【思考力・判断力・表現力】　　共通テスト CD 56

Listen to the English and make the best choice to match the content. (各4点)

1. About how many meters long is each arch of the bridge?

　① Ten　　　　② Thirteen　　　　③ Thirty　　　　④ Ninety

2. What are people likely to buy on the bridge?

　① Beef steak　　② Gold mines　　③ Ruby rings　　④ Smartwatches

3. What is true about the Vasari Corridor?

　① It was built after a row of stores appeared.

　② It was built next to the bridge.

　③ It's not on both sides of the bridge.

　④ Residents of Florence used to walk through it.

In the United States, / the 1970s were still a time / when discrimination against women could be seen / in daily situations. // At that time, / a woman appeared / in court / and **devoted** her life / to fighting against it. //

① On September 18, 2020, / hundreds of people gathered / in front of the U.S. **Supreme** Court / for a moment of silence / after the death of one of its **justices**. // Her name was Ruth Bader Ginsburg, / and she was the second female Supreme Court justice / in history. // She had a strong following / among **liberals**, / women, / and young people / and was given the nickname / "**Notorious** RBG." //

② Ruth was born / in Brooklyn / in 1933 / to a **modest** Jewish family. // When she was a child, / her mother took her / to the library / every week. // It was natural / for women / to stay home / and not work outside the home / in those days, / but Ruth's mother wanted her daughter / to have a proper education / and become an **independent** woman. //

③ In high school, / Ruth was very curious / and tried many things, / including editing the school newspaper, / playing the **cello** / in an **orchestra**, / and **twirling** the **baton**. // Her grades were excellent, / and she was chosen / to speak / at her high school **graduation**. // However, / she didn't attend the graduation ceremony. // The day before the ceremony, / her mother, / who had been struggling / with **cancer**, / had passed away. // (186 words)

🔊 **音読しよう**
    スピーキング・トレーナー

Practice 1   スラッシュ位置で文を区切って読んでみよう ☐
Practice 2   音声を聞きながら，音声のすぐ後を追って読んでみよう ☐
TRY！   １分50秒以内に本文全体を音読しよう ☐

📖 **Reading**   本文の内容を読んで理解しよう【知識・技能】【思考力・判断力・表現力】   共通テスト

Make the correct choice to complete each sentence or answer each question. (各4点)

1. What does "following" in line 7 mean? ☐
   ① attendants   ② enemies   ③ staff   ④ supporters

2. Ruth's mother ☐ .
   ① died the day of Ruth's high school graduation ceremony
   ② was born in Brooklyn in 1933
   ③ wanted Ruth to have a proper education and become an independent woman
   ④ worked for a library

3. Which of the following is **not** true about Ruth Bader Ginsburg? ☐
   ① Her mother took an active role in Ruth's education.
   ② She was a Jewish.

シャドーイングをすることができる。　ギンズバーグ判事の生い立ちに関する英文を読んで，概要や要点を捉えることができる。
文脈を理解して適切な語句を用いて英文を完成することができる。　平易な英語で話される短い英文を聞いて必要な情報を聞き取ることができる。

Goals　尊敬する人物について簡単な語句を用いて説明することができる。　スピーチについて簡単な語句を用いて考えを表現することができる。

③ She was so excellent at high school that she spoke at graduation ceremony.

④ She was the second female U.S. Supreme Court justice.

🔍 Vocabulary & Grammar　重要表現や文法事項について理解しよう【知識】　英検® GTEC®

Make the correct choice to complete each sentence. (各2点)

1. After retiring from teaching, she (　　　) herself to reading ancient documents.
   ① accomplished　　② devoted　　③ engaged　　④ spent

2. He was (　　　) about his accomplishments, although he had much to be proud of.
   ① arrogant　　② modest　　③ remarkable　　④ satisfied

3. Even after we (　　　) away, I believe our souls will continue to live.
   ① give　　② keep　　③ pass　　④ run

4. The city used to be (　　　) as a home of crime and poverty.
   ① fabulous　　② marvelous　　③ notorious　　④ obvious

5. I (　　　) that TV drama every week, but I missed the last episode.
   ① had been watching　　　　② have been watching
   ③ was watching　　　　④ watched

🎧 Listening　英文を聞いて理解しよう【知識・技能】【思考力・判断力・表現力】　共通テスト CD 57

Listen to the English and make the best choice to match the content. (4点)

① Vicky is a high school student who studies hard.

② Vicky made it a rule to study in a school library.

③ Vicky used to go to a library in her high school days.

💬 Interaction　英文を聞いて会話を続けよう【知識・技能】【思考力・判断力・表現力】　スピーキング・トレーナー　CD 58

Listen to the English and respond to the last remark. (7点)

［メモ　　　　　　　　　　　　　　　　　　　　　　　　　　　　　　　　　　］

　アドバイス　理由を付け加えることができる有名人を考えよう。

💬 Production (Speak)　自分の考えを話して伝えよう【思考力・判断力・表現力】　スピーキング・トレーナー

Speak out your answer to the following question. (7点)

If you were chosen to give a graduation speech, what would you talk about?

　アドバイス　卒業式という場にふさわしい内容である必要がある。

----

④ Ruth entered Cornell University / in 1950 / on a full **scholarship**. // At that time, / the number of female students / attending university / was **exceedingly** small. // Eighty percent of her classmates / were male students. // Ruth studied / in secret / because men tended to **dislike intelligent** women. // Then / she met Martin Ginsburg, / who was a year ahead of her / in college. // **Unlike** many other men, / he liked her intelligence. //

⑤ After graduating / from Cornell University / in 1954, / Ruth married Martin, / and they had a daughter. // In 1956, / she entered Harvard Law School, / which her husband was attending. // She had more than 500 classmates, / and only nine of them / were women. // There was no ladies' room / in the main building. // When the building was constructed, / it was not expected / that women would learn law. //

⑥ In her second year, / unfortunately, / Martin was **diagnosed** / with cancer. // Ruth asked his classmates / to take notes / for him / in classes, / and she typed them up / for him / every night. // Without her help, / he could not have graduated. // She continued to work hard / on her studies / while taking care of her husband / and raising their child. // (183 words)

🔊 **音読しよう**　　　　　　　　　　　　　　　　　　　スピーキング・トレーナー

Practice 1　スラッシュ位置で文を区切って読んでみよう □
Practice 2　音声を聞きながら，音声のすぐ後を追って読んでみよう □
TRY !　　　1分50秒以内に本文全体を音読しよう □

📖 **Reading**　本文の内容を読んで理解しよう【知識・技能】【思考力・判断力・表現力】　　共通テスト

Make the correct choice to complete each sentence or answer each question. (各4点)

1. At the time Ruth studied at Cornell University, _____ .
   ① she somehow managed to pay for her education
   ② Martin, her future husband, disliked her at first because of her intelligence
   ③ men tended to get higher scores at exams
   ④ there were fewer female students than male

2. How many women students entered to Harvard Law School in 1956? _____
   ① nine　　　　② twenty　　　　③ eighty　　　　④500

3. Put the events in the order they occurred. _____ → _____ → _____ → _____ → _____
   ① Ruth entered Cornell University.　　② Ruth entered Harvard Law School.
   ③ Ruth married Martin Ginsburg.
   ④ Ruth worked hard while taking care of her husband and raising their child.
   ⑤ Martin was diagnosed with cancer.

●》シャドーイングをすることができる。　　　Ⅲ ギンズバーグ判事の学生時代に関する英文を読んで，概要や要点を捉えることができる。
Q 文脈を理解して適切な語句を用いて英文を完成することができる。　　⌒ 平易な英語で話される短い英文を聞いて必要な情報を聞き取ることができる。
Q 教育について簡単な語句を用いて考えを表現することができる。　　⌒ 男女差別について簡単な語句を用いて考えを表現することができる。

Goals

🔍 Vocabulary & Grammar　重要表現や文法事項について理解しよう【知識】　英検® GTEC®

Make the correct choice to complete each sentence. (各2点)

1. Manufacturing in the country accounted for (　　　) small proportion of the GDP.
   ① an additionally　　② an exceedingly　　③ a previously　　④ a slightly

2. Our hotel stands at the end of the street (　　　) of us.
   ① ahead　　　　② among　　　　③ behind　　　　④ instead

3. I strongly (　　　) cleaning the bathroom because I find it to be a boring task.
   ① alike　　　　② dislike　　　　③ manlike　　　　④ unlike

4. The syndrome has been (　　　) primarily in girls.
   ① diagnosed　　② evaluated　　③ investigated　　④ represented

5. (　　　) a little more practice, Mike would have won the competition.
   ① If　　　　② Unless　　　　③ With　　　　④ Without

🎧 Listening　英文を聞いて理解しよう【知識・技能】【思考力・判断力・表現力】　共通テスト　CD 59

Listen to the English and make the best choice to match the content. (4点)

① Eighteen percent of the students were female fifty years ago.

② The proportion of male students increased over the last fifty years.

③ The percentage of female students fifty years ago was thirty.

💬 Interaction　英文を聞いて会話を続けよう【知識・技能】【思考力・判断力・表現力】　スピーキング・トレーナー　CD 60

Listen to the English and respond to the last remark. (7点)

[メモ　　　　　　　　　　　　　　　　　　　　　　　　　　　　　　　　　　　]

アドバイス　質問されているわけではないが，相手の発言に対する自分の考えを簡単にコメントしよう。

✏️ Production (Write)　自分の考えを書いて伝えよう【思考力・判断力・表現力】

Write your answer to the following question. (7点)

Why did men tend to dislike intelligent women in Ruth's time?

アドバイス　正解があるわけではないので，想像して書いてみよう。

----

⑦ Before she received her **degree** / at Harvard, / her husband got a job / at a law firm / in New York. // The family moved to New York, / and Ruth transferred to Columbia Law School. // She graduated / at the top of her class / in 1959 / and looked for a law firm job. // However, / no firm would **hire** her. // She was female, / had a child, / and was Jewish. //

⑧ She never gave up / looking for a job / and began working / as a law clerk / for a **district** court judge. // In 1963, / she became a professor / at Rutgers Law School. // There, / a female professor earned less / than a male professor. // Ruth, / along with other female **faculty** members, / **sued** the school / and won. // In 1972, / she became the first female **tenured** professor / at Columbia University. //

⑨ Many women / in America / started to speak out / against discrimination against women. // Ruth **co-founded** the Women's Rights Project / in 1972 / at the American Civil **Liberties** Union (ACLU). // She won five / of six **sex**-discrimination cases / before the Supreme Court. // (166 words)

🔊 **音読しよう**　　　　　　　　　　　　　　　　　　　　スピーキング・トレーナー
Practice 1　スラッシュ位置で文を区切って読んでみよう ☐
Practice 2　音声を聞きながら，音声のすぐ後を追って読んでみよう ☐
TRY !　　　　1分40秒以内に本文全体を音読しよう ☐

📖 **Reading**　本文の内容を読んで理解しよう【知識・技能】【思考力・判断力・表現力】　　　共通テスト

Make the correct choice to complete each sentence or answer each question. (各4点)

1. Ruth and her family moved to New York because ☐ .
   ① she gave up studying the law
   ② she got a job at a law firm there
   ③ she graduated and looked for a law firm job
   ④ her husband, Martin, got a job at a law firm there

2. Which of the following is **not** what Ruth did in her early career? ☐
   ① A winner of some sex-discrimination cases
   ② A district court judge
   ③ A professor at Rutgers Law School
   ④ A professor at Columbia University

3. Which organization did Ruth co-found in 1972? ☐
   ① American Civil Liberties Union (ACLU)
   ② Discrimination Against Women Association　　③ Supreme Court
   ④ Women's Rights Project

シャドーイングをすることができる。　　　ギンズバーグ判事の活躍に関する英文を読んで，概要や要点を捉えることができる。
文脈を理解して適切な語句を用いて英文を完成することができる。　　平易な英語で話される短い英文を聞いて必要な情報を聞き取ることができる。
学問について簡単な語句を用いて考えを表現することができる。　　　男女不平等について簡単な語句を用いて考えを表現することができる。

Goals

🔍 Vocabulary & Grammar　重要表現や文法事項について理解しよう【知識】　英検® GTEC®

Make the correct choice to complete each sentence. (各2点)

1. Tell me which medicine I should take. You're the one with a (　　　) in pharmacy.
   ① capacity　　　② degree　　　③ position　　　④ standard

2. In this country, you will find how easy it is to (　　　) someone or a company.
   ① demand　　　② ignore　　　③ offer　　　④ sue

3. His property is in a good farming (　　　) in the Midwest.
   ① district　　　② dominion　　　③ soil　　　④ territory

4. The company had (　　　) a young law student as an intern.
   ① constructed　　　② fired　　　③ hired　　　④ promoted

5. My dog (　　　) not go home even after walking for an hour and a half.
   ① could　　　② might　　　③ should　　　④ would

🎧 Listening　英文を聞いて理解しよう【知識・技能】【思考力・判断力・表現力】　共通テスト CD 61

Listen to the English and make the best choice to match the content. (4点)

① The speaker has a strong will to finish his campus life.

② The speaker hasn't found his job yet.

③ The speaker started to work last week.

💬 Interaction　英文を聞いて会話を続けよう【知識・技能】【思考力・判断力・表現力】　スピーキング・トレーナー CD 62

Listen to the English and respond to the last remark. (7点)

[メモ　　　　　　　　　　　　　　　　　　　　　　　　　　　　　　　　　]

アドバイス　将来の夢につなげて考えてみよう。

✏️ Production (Write)　自分の考えを書いて伝えよう【思考力・判断力・表現力】

Write your answer to the following question. (7点)

Do you feel that gender inequality still exists?

アドバイス　Yes の場合はそれをいつ感じるかなどを補足しよう。

----

⑩ Ruth was **appointed** to the U.S. Court of Appeals / for the District of Columbia / in 1980 / and to the Supreme Court / in 1993. // She always went to **trial** / in support of women's rights, / **anti-racism**, / and **gender equality**. // Ruth wrote many bitter **dissents** / to the Supreme Court's majority opinions / while **conservative** justices had a majority. //

⑪ Ruth's **attitude** encouraged young people / who advocated for equal rights / and social justice. // They started calling Ruth / "Notorious RBG" / after the legendary **rapper**, / "Notorious B.I.G." // T-shirts and coffee cups / with her **portrait**, / **miniature** figures, / and dolls / became popular. // Films / based on her life / have been released. // She was a pop culture icon / as well as a **feminist** icon. //

⑫ When she was diagnosed / with cancer / in 2009, / Ruth returned to work / only nineteen days / after having **surgery**. // When her **beloved** husband died / in 2010, / she **resumed** her job / the next day / because that was what he wanted her / to do. // She continued to fight discrimination / until she died / at the age of 87. // She was, / as her mother had hoped, / a truly independent woman. // (177 words)

🔊 **音読しよう** スピーキング・トレーナー

Practice 1 スラッシュ位置で文を区切って読んでみよう ☐
Practice 2 音声を聞きながら，音声のすぐ後を追って読んでみよう ☐
TRY！ 1分50秒以内に本文全体を音読しよう ☐

📖 **Reading** 本文の内容を読んで理解しよう【知識・技能】【思考力・判断力・表現力】 共通テスト

Make the correct choice to complete each sentence or answer each question. (各4点)

1. What does "support" in line 3 mean? ☐
   ① case   ② favor   ③ front   ④ spite

2. Ruth's supporters started calling her "Notorious RBG" ☐.
   ① after a link to the rapper Notorious B.I.G
   ② after the film based on her life
   ③ as her attitude was infamous among the court
   ④ as she was a fan of Notorious B.I.G

3. Which of the following is **not** true about Ruth's late years? ☐
   ① She came back to her job the next day her husband died.
   ② She died at the age of 87 in 2010.
   ③ She returned to work only nineteen days after having surgery.
   ④ She was fighting cancer.

シャドーイングをすることができる。　　　ギンズバーグ判事の影響力に関する英文を読んで，概要や要点を捉えることができる。
文脈を理解して適切な語句を用いて英文を完成することができる。　　平易な英語で話される短い英文を聞いて必要な情報を聞き取ることができる。
別れについて簡単な語句を用いてコメントすることができる。　　ギンズバーグ判事から学べる事を簡単な語句を用いて表現することができる。

Goals

Vocabulary & Grammar 　重要表現や文法事項について理解しよう【知識】　　英検® GTEC®

Make the correct choice to complete each sentence. (各2点)

1. He was the only voice of (　　　　). There was no one on his side.
   ① against 　　　② dissent 　　　③ opposite 　　　④ trial

2. The Prime Minister (　　　　) one of his old friends to a member of the Cabinet.
   ① appointed 　　　② dismissed 　　　③ engaged 　　　④ indicated

3. Her (　　　　) toward foreigners showed that she was not welcoming them.
   ① attitude 　　　② courtesy 　　　③ presence 　　　④ temper

4. After the sudden rain stopped, we (　　　　) work until dusk.
   ① concluded 　　　② loaded 　　　③ resumed 　　　④ summarized

5. (　　　　) you have any concerns, please contact us.
   ① Could 　　　② Do 　　　③ Should 　　　④ Would

Listening 　英文を聞いて理解しよう【知識・技能】【思考力・判断力・表現力】　　共通テスト CD 63

Listen to the English and make the best choice to match the content. (4点)

① He will have to pay $10,000 to the company.

② His claim gained agreement without any dissent.

③ The company has just agreed to his demand.

Interaction 　英文を聞いて会話を続けよう【知識・技能】【思考力・判断力・表現力】　　スピーキング・トレーナー CD 64

Listen to the English and respond to the last remark. (7点)

[メモ 　　]

アドバイス 　相手に共感するコメントをしよう。

Production (Write) 　自分の考えを書いて伝えよう【思考力・判断力・表現力】

Write your answer to the following question. (7点)

What have you learned from Ruth's life?

アドバイス 　Lesson 9 全体を通して考えよう。

You're looking at an online article / about Ruth Bader Ginsburg's ACLU-era trials. //

Ruth didn't just **insist** on women's rights. // She believed / all genders should be given equal rights. // That **belief** is reflected / in the trials / she was involved in / as a lawyer. //

In a 1973 Supreme Court case, / for example, / she **defended** a female **lieutenant** / who was treated differently / from her male colleagues. // At the time, / male service members were receiving / housing and medical benefits / for their **spouses**. // However, / when the lieutenant applied for the same benefits, / she was **denied** them / because she was a woman / and her spouse was a man. // **Federal** law stated / that only female service members had to prove / that their husbands depended on them. // Male service members' wives automatically became dependents. // The justices, / who were all men, / **initially** couldn't understand / that this law was **discriminatory**. // Ruth convinced them / that treating men and women differently / because of gender / became discrimination. // As a result, / she won the trial / by a vote of 8-1. //

A trial / in 1975 / is also an excellent example / of Ruth's thinking. // A woman died / during **childbirth**. // Her husband decided / to raise their son / and went to the local Social Security office / to ask about **parental** benefits. // However, / he learned / that he couldn't apply for the benefit / because he was a man. // Under the social security law / at that time, / only mothers could get it. // In the Supreme Court, / Ruth insisted / it was **unconstitutional** / to **withhold** benefits / because of gender. // In the end, / she won the trial. //

In another trial / in 1979, / Ruth pointed out / that the **jury selection** process / involved discrimination. // At the time, / jury duty was **optional** / for women / in several states, / while it was **compulsory** / for men. // Some women might have been grateful / for the rule / because **fulfilling** the duty was a **burden**. // However, / Ruth argued / that jury duty should be compulsory / for women / as well as men. // She thought / that women's service / on juries / should be seen to be as valuable / as that of men. //

Through the cases / in which she was involved, / Ruth showed / that there was gender-based discrimination / in the law / and that it hurt everyone. // She didn't want women / to have special rights. // She thought / that everyone should be equal / **regardless** of gender. //

(364 words)

🔊 音読しよう

スピーキング・トレーナー

Practice 1 　スラッシュ位置で文を区切って読んでみよう ☐
Practice 2 　音声を聞きながら，音声のすぐ後を追って読んでみよう ☐
TRY！　　　３分40秒以内に本文全体を音読しよう ☐

📖 Reading　本文の内容を読んで理解しよう【知識・技能】【思考力・判断力・表現力】　共通テスト

Make the correct choice to complete each sentence or answer each question. (各5点)

1. Ruth believed that _____.

　① jury duty should be optional for men as well as women

　② men shouldn't apply for the parental benefits

　③ treating men and women differently because of gender was discrimination

　④ women should be given special rights

2. Which is the most suitable title for the article? _____

　① Ruth Bader Ginsburg — An Advocate for Gender Equality

　② The Justices Who Fought for Women's Rights

　③ The Social Security Law that Changed Society

　④ The Trials that Ruth Bader Ginsburg Won

🔍 Vocabulary & Grammar　重要表現や文法事項について理解しよう【知識】　英検® GTEC®

Make the correct choice to complete each sentence. (各3点)

1. My friend accidentally got (　　) in a bank robbery.

　① done　　　　　② involved　　　　③ started　　　　④ tired

2. She (　　) for and received the post of a region manager.

　① applied　　　　② insisted　　　　③ required　　　　④ urged

3. In Japan, education is (　　) up to the end of junior high school.

　① advisory　　　　② compulsory　　　③ ordinary　　　④ voluntary

4. We are committed to equal employment opportunity (　　) of age, race, or gender.

　① despite　　　　② nevertheless　　　③ no matter　　　④ regardless

5. She has several hobbies (　　) I have only one.

　① as　　　　　　② for　　　　　　③ which　　　　　④ while

🎧 Listening　英文を聞いて理解しよう【知識・技能】【思考力・判断力・表現力】　共通テスト 🔘CD 65

Listen to the English and make the best choice to match the content. (各5点)

1. What did Lilly demand in the trial?

　① Additional payment　　　　　　② Pay discrimination

　③ Refund　　　　　　　　　　　　④ Retirement money

2. How many justices disagree with Lilly's appeal?

　① Four　　　　　② Five　　　　　③ Eight　　　　④ Nine

3. Why did they turn down Lilly's appeal?

　① Because Ruth supported Lilly in the trial.

　② Because she didn't meet the deadline.

　③ Because she left Goodyear Company.

　④ Because the government didn't pass a new law.

Tatsuya Miyo was involved / in a car accident / at the age of eighteen. // At that time, / as a **teenager**, / he often wondered, / "What is the meaning / of my life?" //

① I found myself / lying on a bed. // According to the doctor, / I suffered a **cervical** spinal cord injury / when I **collided** head-on with a car / on my **motorbike**. // After a few months / of **rehabilitation**, / I thought, / "If I have to stay / in a wheelchair / for the rest of my life, / it will be over." //

② After moving from hospital to hospital, / I finally entered / a rehabilitation **facility** / in Shizuoka Prefecture. // There, / I met a middle-aged man / who had the same **disability**. // He gave me **precious** advice, / and I started / to think of him / as my **mentor**. // Thanks to his advice, / I gradually came to feel positive / about my situation. //

③ When I was wondering / about how to live my life, / **fond** memories of traveling / came to mind. // I had an idea / to plan a trip / that could help others / who are in a similar difficult situation / to mine. // Since I first went abroad / to Hawaii / at the age of 23, / my **outlook** on life / had changed **dramatically**. // In the summer / when I was 28, / I set off / on a nine-month **journey** / around the world / by myself, / sharing my travel experiences / in a wheelchair / as well as overseas **barrier-free** information. // (197 words)

🔊 **音読しよう**　　　　　　　　　　　　　　　　　　　　　スピーキング・トレーナー
Practice 1　スラッシュ位置で文を区切って読んでみよう ☐
Practice 2　音声を聞きながら，音声のすぐ後を追って読んでみよう ☐
TRY！　　　2分以内に本文全体を音読しよう ☐

📖 **Reading**　本文の内容を読んで理解しよう【知識・技能】【思考力・判断力・表現力】　　共通テスト

Make the correct choice to complete each sentence or answer each question. (各4点)

1. Which of the following is true about the accident that Tatsuya was involved in? ☐
   ① Tatsuya and the other's motorbikes collided with each other.
   ② Tatsuya crashed into a car on his motorbike.
   ③ Tatsuya was driving a car and hit a motorbike.
   ④ Tatsuya was hit by a car when walking.

2. Thanks to the mentor Tatsuya met at a rehabilitation facility, he ☐ .
   ① became confident with his remaining physical abilities
   ② came to feel positive about his situation
   ③ made up his mind to become a doctor
   ④ took a first step toward a journey around the world

3.　Tatsuya set off on a nine-month journey around the world when he was ☐ .

　①18　　　　　　　②20　　　　　　　③23　　　　　　　④28

◯ **Vocabulary & Grammar**　　重要表現や文法事項について理解しよう【知識】　　　　英検® GTEC®

Make the correct choice to complete each sentence. (各2点)

1.　I nearly (　　　　) with a girl in the classroom.

　① agreed　　　　　② collided　　　　　③ missed　　　　　④ swept

2.　Merging two companies was a big (　　　　), but we managed to make it happen.

　① journey　　　　　② tour　　　　　③ travel　　　　　④ trip

3.　She cherishes the moment she first held her (　　　) newborn baby.

　① expensive　　　　② luxurious　　　　③ offensive　　　　④ precious

4.　The girl gave the new student a (　　　) look.

　① concerning　　　② fond　　　　　　③ partial　　　　　④ silly

5.　Please leave the windows (　　　) when you go to bed.

　① be locked　　　　② lock　　　　　　③ locked　　　　　④ to lock

◯ **Listening**　　英文を聞いて理解しよう【知識・技能】【思考力・判断力・表現力】　　　共通テスト　CD ◎ 66

Listen to the English and make the best choice to match the content. (4点)

　① The speaker learned how to work in the facility.

　② The speaker spent a few years away from home.

　③ The speaker walked to the facility from his house.

◯ **Interaction**　　英文を聞いて会話を続けよう【知識・技能】【思考力・判断力・表現力】　　スピーキング・トレーナー　CD ◎ 67

Listen to the English and respond to the last remark. (7点)

　[メモ　　　　　　　　　　　　　　　　　　　　　　　　　　　　　　　　　]

　アドバイス　自分より年上，もしくは経験が豊富で，あなたに助言をくれるような人を挙げよう。

◯ **Production (Speak)**　　自分の考えを話して伝えよう【思考力・判断力・表現力】　　スピーキング・トレーナー

Speak out your answer to the following question. (7点)

　Do you see any barrier-free design in your neighborhood?

　アドバイス　身近な例を挙げよう。

④ Soon after I set out, / a **scam** group stole 50,000 yen / from me / at the Louvre Museum / in Paris. // When I returned to my hotel / in shock, / I talked with a clerk, / whom later I nicknamed Pierre. // "I'm shocked. // I'll hate Paris / because of the trouble / at the Louvre." // He listened to me carefully / and gave me / his contact information. //

⑤ The next morning, / I got an email / from Pierre: / "We decided / to serve you breakfast / for free." // I almost cried / and **thankfully** replied, / "Why don't we go / for dinner?" // Then / I got an **unexpected** message: / "Let's go / to the Louvre / again." // I was reluctant to go, / but I really enjoyed the museum / with Pierre's **humorous explanation**. // After leaving there / in the evening, / Pierre looked up / at the night sky / and said, / "I wanted to change your sad Louvre / into a **memorable** one." // His words shook my heart. //

⑥ The incident / at the Louvre / certainly made me feel **negatively** / about Paris, / but thanks to Pierre, / I left Paris / with good memories. // Even if you face something / you don't like, / you may still get a good impression / about it / afterwards / as long as you don't stick to the first impression. // What I learned from Pierre / had a great influence / on my way of thinking. // (211 words)

🔊 **音読しよう**　　　　　　　　　　　　　　　　　　スピーキング・トレーナー
Practice 1　スラッシュ位置で文を区切って読んでみよう □
Practice 2　音声を聞きながら，音声のすぐ後を追って読んでみよう □
TRY !　　　2分10秒以内に本文全体を音読しよう □

📖 **Reading**　本文の内容を読んで理解しよう【知識・技能】【思考力・判断力・表現力】　　共通テスト

Make the correct choice to complete each sentence or answer each question. (各4点)

1. Put the events in the order they occurred. ☐ → ☐ → ☐ → ☐ → ☐

① Pierre gave Tatsuya his contact information.

② Pierre invited Tatsuya to free breakfast.

③ Tatsuya and Pierre went to the Louvre Museum together.

④ Tatsuya had his money stolen at the Louvre Museum.

⑤ Tatsuya was touched by Pierre's words.

2. Why was the message from Pierre asking Tatsuya to go to the Louvre together unexpected to Tatsuya? ☐

① Because it was a place with bad memories for Tatsuya and Pierre knew it.

② Because Pierre was going to have a clerk job on the day.

③ Because Tatsuya expected Pierre to have dinner together.

④ Because Tatsuya had other places he wanted to visit.

◀》 シャドーイングをすることができる。　　　　　　⚏ パリでの三代さんに関する英文を読んで，概要や要点を捉えることができる。
⌕ 文脈を理解して適切な語句を用いて英文を完成することができる。　　🎧 平易な英語で話される短い英文を聞いて必要な情報を聞き取ることができる。
💬 落とし物について簡単な語句を用いて説明することができる。　　　　✐ 心に残る言葉について簡単な語句を用いて考えを表現することができる。

Goals

3. Tatsuya learned from Pierre that ⬚ .

　　① bad impressions can be changed to good ones depending on your mindset

　　② if you face something you don't like, turn around and run away

　　③ the Louvre was not as good as Tatsuya had expected

　　④ travelers must always be careful of crime

🔍 Vocabulary & Grammar　　重要表現や文法事項について理解しよう【知識】　　英検◎ GTEC◎

Make the correct choice to complete each sentence. (各2点)

1. Hey, kids! Look at this mess! Don't you think you owe me an (　　　)?
　　① advice　　　　　　② explanation　　　　③ intention　　　　④ obedience

2. People around the world reacted in (　　　) when the singer died in his thirties.
　　① particular　　　　② shock　　　　　　③ total　　　　　④ vain

3. Never speak (　　　) to your child about his or her friends.
　　① exceptionally　　② dramatically　　　③ negatively　　　④ thankfully

4. You can borrow my car, as (　　　) as you promise to return it by tomorrow.
　　① far　　　　　　　② long　　　　　　　③ much　　　　　④ well

5. Don't trust him. He is the (　　　) reliable person I have ever met.
　　① last　　　　　　　② latest　　　　　　③ least　　　　　④ worst

🎧 Listening　　英文を聞いて理解しよう【知識・技能】【思考力・判断力・表現力】　　共通テスト　CD 68

Listen to the English and make the best choice to match the content. (4点)

　　① The speaker dropped the earring on the road.

　　② The speaker gave a kindness to a stranger.

　　③ The speaker got a new earring.

💬 Interaction　　英文を聞いて会話を続けよう【知識・技能】【思考力・判断力・表現力】　スピーキング・トレーナー　CD 69

Listen to the English and respond to the last remark. (7点)

　　［メモ　　　　　　　　　　　　　　　　　　　　　　　　　　　　　　　　 ］

　　アドバイス　Yes の場合は，そのときの状況や気持ちを描写しよう。

✐ Production (Write)　　自分の考えを書いて伝えよう【思考力・判断力・表現力】

Write your answer to the following question. (7点)

　　What are the words or phrases that moved your heart?

　　アドバイス　具体的な言葉を挙げて，その理由を付け加えよう。

⑦ When I traveled / to Athens, / **Greece**, / I met a man / who had come from India. // During my visit / to the Parthenon, / he kindly gave me support, / which was beyond my **expectation**. // When I asked the man / what made him so kind, / he replied, / "We were all born / and grew up / in this universe. // Gender, / age, / and disability / don't matter / at all. // I just had time / today / to help you. // Thank you / for giving me / such a wonderful day." //

⑧ On hearing his words, / I realized / it was **incorrect** / to **assume** / that others would mind helping me / with my disability. // Before I started traveling, / I felt / it was sad and **inconvenient** / to be **confined** / to a wheelchair. // What I learned / during my travel / to Athens / was very simple: / I can stay / just the way I am. //

⑨ Now, / I want to create an environment / where everyone can enjoy traveling. // If your life is boring / with daily **routines**, / traveling will give you a **departure** / from your normal life. // Take a step / forward / and experience something unusual / by making changes / yourself. // If you do that, / I believe / you can grow / by thinking about your life, / **relying** on others / and studying by yourself. // (197 words)

🔊 **音読しよう**　　　　　　　　　　　　　　　　　　　スピーキング・トレーナー
Practice 1　スラッシュ位置で文を区切って読んでみよう☐
Practice 2　音声を聞きながら，音声のすぐ後を追って読んでみよう☐
TRY！　　　2分以内に本文全体を音読しよう☐

📖 **Reading**　本文の内容を読んで理解しよう【知識・技能】【思考力・判断力・表現力】　　共通テスト

Make the correct choice to complete each sentence or answer each question. (各4点)

1. What does "assume" in line 7 mean? ☐
    ① conclude　　　　② doubt　　　　③ prove　　　　④ suppose

2. In Athens, Tatsuya learned that ☐ .
    ① a wheelchair traveler can give people a wonderful day
    ② it is all right to be the way he is
    ③ visiting various places in wheelchair is not difficult as it looks
    ④ we can meet people from different countries anywhere on earth

3. What does Tatsuya suggest to people whose lives are boring with daily routines? ☐
    ① To create an environment where everyone can enjoy traveling.
    ② To experience something unusual.
    ③ To rely on others.　　　　　　　　④ To think about your life.

🔍 Vocabulary & Grammar　重要表現や文法事項について理解しよう【知識】　英検® GTEC®

Make the correct choice to complete each sentence. (各2点)

1. The illegally captured animals were (　　　) to small cages.
   ① allowed　　② confined　　③ put　　④ released
2. (　　　) hanging up the phone, she heard the doorbell ring.
   ① At　　② For　　③ On　　④ To
3. The sporting event largely (　　　) on volunteer workers.
   ① commits　　② insists　　③ reflects　　④ relies
4. She didn't like her mother calling and interrupting her morning (　　　).
   ① order　　② routine　　③ technique　　④ usage
5. Cathy is the (　　　) person who would tell a lie.
   ① last　　② late　　③ latest　　④ least

🎧 Listening　英文を聞いて理解しよう【知識・技能】【思考力・判断力・表現力】　共通テスト　CD 70

Listen to the English and make the best choice to match the content. (4点)

① The man had trouble because of other passengers.
② The speaker gave help to the man all alone.
③ The speaker helped the man get off the bus.

💬 Interaction　英文を聞いて会話を続けよう【知識・技能】【思考力・判断力・表現力】　スピーキング・トレーナー　CD 71

Listen to the English and respond to the last remark. (7点)

［メ　モ　　　　　　　　　　　　　　　　　　　　　　　　　　　　　　　　］

アドバイス　相手の発言のように例を描写しよう。

✏️ Production (Write)　自分の考えを書いて伝えよう【思考力・判断力・表現力】

Write your answer to the following question. (7点)

If you feel your life is boring with daily routines, what would you like to start?

アドバイス　routine とは逆の「非日常」に感じる例を挙げよう。

95

⑩ After suffering my injury, / I sometimes wanted to die, / but now / I'm glad / I am alive. // When you feel like **isolating** yourself / from society, / it's a great adventure / for you / to step outside. // Traveling is a life textbook / with no printed pages. // The content of the textbook is different, / depending on your stage / in life, / and is always changing. //

⑪ I cherished three ideas / I had learned / from my mentor / — **encounter**, / challenge / and action. // Meet someone / and discover a new sense of values / that you hadn't noticed / on your own. // By taking on challenges, / you **accumulate** small successful experiences / and gain **confidence**. // The experience / gained through encounters / and the confidence / **cultivated** through repeated challenges / will broaden the range of your actions / in the world. //

⑫ A friend of mine / in Hawaii / gave me a wonderful phrase: / "No Rain, / No Rainbow." // Anyone can feel down / when it rains. // However, / don't forget / that the rain is necessary / for you / to fully enjoy the rainbow / of happiness / that follows. // I believe / bad things will often change / into better things / afterwards. // If something **unpleasant** happens, / you can think / "That was a necessary rain" / in the end. // (191 words)

🔊 **音読しよう**　　　スピーキング・トレーナー

Practice 1　スラッシュ位置で文を区切って読んでみよう □
Practice 2　音声を聞きながら，音声のすぐ後を追って読んでみよう □
TRY！　　　2分以内に本文全体を音読しよう □

📖 **Reading**　本文の内容を読んで理解しよう【知識・技能】【思考力・判断力・表現力】　共通テスト

Make the correct choice to complete each sentence or answer each question. (各4点)

1. According to Tatsuya, traveling is a _____.
   ① great adventure to give you an opportunity to isolate yourself from society
   ② great adventure for those who are suffering injury
   ③ life textbook that always tells you what to do next
   ④ life textbook whose contents are always changing

2. Which of the following is **not** included in the three ideas Tatsuya cherishes? _____
   ① action　　② challenge　　③ encounter　　④ discover

3. One **fact** from paragraph 12 is that _____.
   ① a friend of Tatsuya gave him a phrase　② anyone feel down when it rains
   ③ bad things will change into better things afterwards
   ④ rain is necessary to fully enjoy the rainbow of happiness that follows

Vocabulary & Grammar　重要表現や文法事項について理解しよう【知識】　　英検® GTEC®

Make the correct choice to complete each sentence. (各2点)

1. Jesse got the feeling he'd be (　　　　) on more than he could handle.

   ① counting　　　② keeping　　　③ relying　　　④ taking

2. Donald tried to forget the (　　　　) questions asked by interviewers that day.

   ① admiring　　　② meaningful　　　③ precious　　　④ unpleasant

3. Since she had a sore throat, she stayed home to (　　　　) herself from work.

   ① express　　　② isolate　　　③ preserve　　　④ withstand

4. All the evidence (　　　　) over the years turned out to be false.

   ① accumulated　　② increased　　③ lessened　　④ spread

5. His Spanish was (　　　　) but perfect.

   ① anything　　　② everything　　　③ nothing　　　④ something

Listening　英文を聞いて理解しよう【知識・技能】【思考力・判断力・表現力】　共通テスト　CD 72

Listen to the English and make the best choice to match the content. (4点)

   ① Joe made the speaker realize something important.

   ② Joe noticed the importance of keeping doing something like the speaker.

   ③ Joe probably decided to travel with the speaker.

Interaction　英文を聞いて会話を続けよう【知識・技能】【思考力・判断力・表現力】　スピーキング・トレーナー　CD 73

Listen to the English and respond to the last remark. (7点)

   [メモ　　　　　　　　　　　　　　　　　　　　　　　　　　　　　　　]

   アドバイス　共感を求められている。

Production (Write)　自分の考えを書いて伝えよう【思考力・判断力・表現力】

Write your answer to the following question. (7点)

   Have you ever experienced "a necessary rain" like Tatsuya did?

   アドバイス　「必要な雨」とはどんな雨だろうか。これまでを振り返って思い出してみよう。

You found an interview article / about Yui Kamiji / on the Internet. //

Yui Kamiji

Date of birth: April 24, 1994   Country: Japan   Sport: Wheelchair Tennis

Yui Kamiji started wheelchair tennis / at the age of 11 / and was ranked No.1 / in Japan / at the age of 14. // She played / in the London 2012 Paralympic Games / in her third year / of high school / and was finally ranked No.1 / in the world / in 2014. // In the Tokyo 2020 Paralympics, / she won / the silver medal. // Let's learn / about her story. //

■ Interview //

I was originally able to walk / with **orthoses**, / but as I grew up, / it became harder / for me / to walk. // Despite facing difficulties / ever since I was a child, / if I was going to do something, / I wanted to do it / under the same conditions / as everyone else. // For example, / when I was in elementary school, / my teacher said / that I could not take part / in a relay race / because I might trip / and hurt myself / if I ran. // This really **annoyed** me. // I thought / it should be the same / for everyone. // Why was I the only one / who could not take part / in the race? //

Since I was very young, / my parents / and others close to me / created an environment / where I could try anything / I wanted to do. // They respected my wishes. // I am very grateful for that. // I learned the importance / of clearly **conveying** to others / what I wanted to do / and what I could do / myself, / and also / of asking others / for their help and **cooperation** / when necessary. // I also learned / the importance / of understanding how many people had helped me / to get to where I am, / and of feeling gratitude / toward them. // These ideas became an important part / of my identity. // It is about / how I should be / as a person, / which comes before / how I should be / as an athlete, / and I think of that / every day. //

(295 words)

🔊 音読しよう   スピーキング・トレーナー

Practice 1   スラッシュ位置で文を区切って読んでみよう ☐
Practice 2   音声を聞きながら，音声のすぐ後を追って読んでみよう ☐
TRY！   3分以内に本文全体を音読しよう ☐

📖 **Reading**   本文の内容を読んで理解しよう 【知識・技能】【思考力・判断力・表現力】   共通テスト

Make the correct choice to answer each question. (各5点)

1. Which of the following is **not** true about Yui Kamiji's record as an athlete? ☐
    ① She was ranked No.1 in Japan at the age of 14.

② She played in the London 2012 Paralympics in her third year of high school.

③ She was ranked No.1 in the world in 2014.

④ She won the gold medal in the Tokyo 2020 Paralympics.

2. What important life lessons did Yui learn from her experiences and the support of her parents and others close to her? 　

① The importance of participating in sports competitions.

② The need to prioritize her identity as an athlete over her identity as a person.

③ The significance of respecting others' wishes and desires.

④ The value of feeling grateful and expressing gratitude to those who have helped her.

Vocabulary & Grammar　重要表現や文法事項について理解しよう【知識】　英検® GTEC®

Make the correct choice to complete each sentence. (各3点)

1. The company has more than 800 employees, including the (　　　) hired 5 people.
   ① hopefully　② originally　③ technically　④ voluntarily

2. The ambassador (　　　) the greetings of the King to the President.
   ① conveyed　② hid　③ refused　④ revealed

3. That bump on the road is dangerous. Someone might (　　) over it.
   ① beat　② catch　③ trip　④ roll

4. Boarding a crowded train always (　　) me. I wish I could drive a car.
   ① annoys　② comforts　③ teases　④ worries

5. She deserves (　　) for the contribution she has made.
   ① curiosity　② frustration　③ gratitude　④ punishment

6. This film was made with the (　　) of the United Nations.
   ① alliance　② cooperation　③ harmony　④ obstruction

Listening　英文を聞いて理解しよう【知識・技能】【思考力・判断力・表現力】　共通テスト CD 74

Listen to the English and make the best choice to match the content. (各4点)

1. What do volunteer students do during the lecture?
   ① Set up a laptop computer for Mizuki.　② Show textbooks to Mizuki.
   ③ Support Mizuki writing a report.　④ Type what the teacher says.

2. Who can ask a question with a smartphone?
   ① Mizuki　② Staff　③ Teachers　④ Volunteers

3. Where does Mizuki usually eat lunch with her friends?
   ① At a cafeteria　② In a classroom
   ③ In a convenience store　④ In a fast-food restaurant

WANTED //

University student / to sit / with elderly woman //

between 3 and 6 p.m., // Monday through Friday //

Peter Brent needed money / and was ready / to do / any kind of work. // When he read the newspaper advertisement / he decided / he could even sit / three hours a day / with an elderly woman / if necessary. //

Peter rang the bell. // In a few seconds / a young woman / in a black uniform / opened the door. //

"I've come about the advertisement," / Peter told her. // The young woman looked at him / rather strangely. // "I'll tell Ms. Marvin," / she said, / and disappeared. //

A moment later / a woman / in her late thirties / appeared. // "There must be some mistake," / she said. //

"It's about your advertisement / in the newspaper," / Peter explained. //

"Yes, / I know, / but you see, / we wanted a woman / for the position, / not a man." //

"The notice simply said / 'university student.' " //

"I'm terribly sorry, / but we really need a woman / to care for my mother." //

At that moment / a woman in a wheelchair / entered from another room. // She seemed quite old / but sat in her chair / with great **dignity**, / rather like a queen. // "Who is this, / Celia?" // she asked, / pointing at Peter. //

"He's come about the position / we discussed, / Mother, / someone / to stay with you / when I'm out." //

"I've told you / a hundred times, / Celia, / I'm not a baby! // I don't need to be sat with." //

"Mother, / we've talked that / all over. // You can't be here / alone / for three hours / every afternoon. // The servants are busy / and ...." //

"And you have to play cards / and talk with your friends!" //

"Mother!" //

"Well, / it's true." //

"I've just told the young man / we want a woman / for this position." //

"Why? // Listen to me, / Celia. // I'm the one / to decide / who is going to stay with me / —— if anyone is." //

"I really think, / Mother ...." // (302 words)

🔊 **音読しよう**

Practice 1 スラッシュ位置で文を区切って読んでみよう ☐

Practice 2 音声を聞きながら，音声のすぐ後を追って読んでみよう ☐

TRY! 3分以内に本文全体を音読しよう ☐

スピーキング・トレーナー

📖 Reading　本文の内容を読んで理解しよう【知識・技能】【思考力・判断力・表現力】　　　共通テスト

Make the correct choice to complete each sentence or answer each question. (各6点)

1. The young woman who opened the door looked at Peter rather strangely because
　　　　.

　① he arrived three hours earlier than she expected

　② he didn't look like a university student

　③ she didn't know about the advertisement

　④ she expected a woman to come for the position

2. Why did Celia post the advertisement on a newspaper? 　　　

　① Because her mother wanted friends to talk with.

　② Because she needed someone to be with her mother while she was out.

　③ Because she needed someone to play cards with.

　④ Because the servants were busy and more workers were needed.

3. Which of the following is most suitable to follow "if anyone is" in line 32? 　　　

　① going to catch me　　　　　　　② going to decide

　③ going to sit with me　　　　　　④ going to take me up

🔍 Vocabulary　重要表現について理解しよう【知識】　　　英検® GTEC®

Make the correct choice to complete each sentence. (各3点)

1. We discussed what to do if our mom should become unable to (　　　) herself.

　① care for　　　　② handle with　　　③ stand for　　　④ take care

2. Death with (　　　) is legalized in some countries.

　① capacity　　　　② dignity　　　　③ sanitary　　　④ tendency

3. The police are searching for a man (　　　) his 40s or 50s.

　① at　　　　　　② for　　　　　　③ in　　　　　　④ of

4. His face on wanted lists are posted (　　　) the town.

　① all over　　　　② everywhere　　　③ in every　　　④ overall

5. What present, if (　　　), did you get from them yesterday?

　① any　　　　　　② ever　　　　　　③ not　　　　　　④ some

✏️ Production (Write)　自分の考えを書いて伝えよう【思考力・判断力・表現力】

Write your answer to the following question. (7点)

　Do you want to work while you are a student? Or have you worked?

　アドバイス　現時点で働いたことがない場合は自分が大学生になったらしてみたいアルバイトなどを想像してみよう。

"All right! // If you insist / that I have a **sitter** / I'll take him!" // She pointed at Peter / again. // "After all, / it's my money / that's going to be paid, / so I decide / who's going to be here. // What's your name, / young man?" //

"Peter Brent." //

"Well, / Peter, / if you're going to work / here, / why not start / now? // Come along! // Push me / into the next room. // We'll discuss / what you have to do / in private." // Peter looked at Ms. Marvin / but she only looked back / as if to say / "What can I do?" //

So / Peter took the job / — rather, / the job took Peter! // Five minutes after being told / he wouldn't do / he found himself working. //

"I forgot / to introduce myself. // I am Ms. Arthur Carlyle," / she said / "and this room is my little world." //

She began / to tell Peter / about herself, / and there was much / to tell / — about her dead husband, / her three children, / now all married, / and her life / until now. // Peter decided / he was going to like Ms. Carlyle, / although at the same time / he was just a bit afraid / of her, / too. /

"So, / young man, / you know all / about me," / she said, / "and what about you? // If you're going to be here / three hours / every day / there are things / for me / to know about you, / too." /

Peter gave Ms. Carlyle a short history / of himself. // "I'm in my last year / of university," / he finished, / "studying English Literature. // I want to be a teacher." //

"You won't get rich, / but that isn't important, / you know. // Arthur and I were happiest / when we had nothing / but each other." // Ms. Carlyle smiled / for the first time. // "I like you, / Peter Brent, / but then I knew / immediately I was going to." //

"I'm glad, / but how did you know?" // (295 words)

🔊 **音読しよう**　　　　　　　　　　　　　　　　　　　スピーキング・トレーナー

Practice 1　スラッシュ位置で文を区切って読んでみよう ☐
Practice 2　音声を聞きながら，音声のすぐ後を追って読んでみよう ☐
TRY!　　　3分以内に本文全体を音読しよう ☐

📖 **Reading**　本文の内容を読んで理解しよう【知識・技能】【思考力・判断力・表現力】　　共通テスト

Make the correct choice to complete each sentence or answer each question. (各6点)

1. What does "the job took Peter" mean in line 9? ☐

　① Getting the position was decided by Ms. Carlyle all of a sudden.

② Peter was chosen as he was the most excellent candidate.

③ Peter was reluctant to get the position but had no choice.

④ Peter was the only applicant for the position.

2. Which of the following is **not** true about Ms. Arthur Carlyle? 〔　　〕

① She had three children and all of them were married.

② She asked Peter to introduce himself after she had done so.

③ She took Peter as her sitter and told him to start working the next day.

④ She was happiest when she was with her husband, even though they were not rich.

3. One **fact** about the story is that 〔　　〕.

① being a teacher wouldn't make Peter rich

② Peter knew all about Ms. Carlyle after her self-introduction

③ Peter was a senior in university who wanted to be a teacher

④ Ms. Carlyle and her husband had nothing but each other

🔍 Vocabulary　重要表現について理解しよう【知識】　　　　英検 ® GTEC®

Make the correct choice to complete each sentence. (各3点)

1. When Sue talked about her fond memories of her parents, she cried and laughed at (　　　).

   ① least　　　② most　　　③ the time　　　④ the same time

2. (　　　) go for a walk together?

   ① How about　　② What about　　③ Why don't　　④ Why not

3. Don't leave your house without hiring a cat (　　　).

   ① breeder　　② groomer　　③ owner　　④ sitter

4. Ted's teacher gave him some advice in (　　　) to handle his friendship problems.

   ① fact　　② private　　③ shock　　④ total

5. Recently I often find myself (　　　) about him.

   ① having thought　② thinking　③ thought　④ to think

✏ Production (Write)　自分の考えを書いて伝えよう【思考力・判断力・表現力】

Write your answer to the following question. (7点)

Try to introduce yourself as if you were in Peter's position.

アドバイス　自分の趣味や好きな教科，将来の夢などを交えて書いてみるとよいでしょう。

"I'm an old woman. // I've lived many years / and met many people, / good and bad. // A young man / who will sit / with a **dull**, demanding old woman / day after day / because he wants money / to study and become a teacher / has to have some good / in him. // Also …" / her voice suddenly turned soft, / "you remind me / of my Arthur. // He looked very much like you / when I married him." //

"Now, / what is it / you're to do / when you come?" / she asked / finally. //

"I have no idea. // Ms. Marvin didn't tell me." //

The old lady laughed. // "I didn't give her time. // Well, / we have plans to make / then / and we'll make them / as we wish. // I suppose, / Peter, / you had some idea / of sitting here / every day / and studying / while I slept / in my chair. // Right?" //

"Well, / I …." //

"Wrong! // Why should you sit here / with the writing of Shakespeare, / Thackeray / and Dickens / to enjoy all by yourself / day after day / and not share them / with me? // I've never had a chance / to study them, / but as they say, / you're never too old / to learn." //

"You mean / you want me to read / to you?" //

"No, / Peter. // That takes too long. // I've still got good eyes / and can read. // Tell me / what you're working on; / I'll read it / in the morning / and we can talk about it / in the afternoon. // How does that seem?" //

"Fine." // What else was there / to say / but "Fine"? // After all, / he was going to be paid / to come here / every day. // He had some doubts, / however. // What use was it going to be / to discuss English Literature / with an old woman / in a wheelchair? //

"Where do we begin?" / asked Ms. Carlyle, / her eyes already bright / with **excitement**. //

"Well, / for our next class / we will compare the characters / of King Lear and Hamlet. // Whose life was more **tragic**?" // (311 words)

🔊 音読しよう スピーキング・トレーナー

Practice 1 スラッシュ位置で文を区切って読んでみよう ☐

Practice 2 音声を聞きながら，音声のすぐ後を追って読んでみよう ☐

TRY! 3分10秒以内に本文全体を音読しよう ☐

📖 **Reading** 本文の内容を読んで理解しよう【知識・技能】【思考力・判断力・表現力】 共通テスト

Make the correct choice to complete each sentence or answer each question. (各6点)

1. Which of the following are the reasons that Ms. Carlyle immediately liked Peter?

(Choose two options. The order does not matter.)　☐ ・ ☐

① She found a good person in young student who would sit with an old woman.

② She knew that whoever wanted to become a teacher was nice.

③ She saw her husband's image in him.

④ She wanted someone who Ms. Marvin didn't want.

2. What does "Wrong!" mean in line 12?　☐

① Ms. Carlyle's doubt against Peter's intention on his work time.

② That Ms. Carlyle never slept in her wheelchair.

③ Peter's idea of studying while the old lady was asleep.

④ Peter's idea that Ms. Carlyle knew nothing about literature.

3. Ms. Carlyle and Peter were probably going to ☐ in their first afternoon.

① discuss the characters in Shakespeare's works

② make plans for their afternoons as they wish

③ sleep in chair

④ read aloud the works of Shakespeare, Thackeray and Dickens

🔍 **Vocabulary**　重要表現について理解しよう【知識】　英検® GTEC®

Make the correct choice to complete each sentence. (各3点)

1. The children's eyes lit up with (　　) when the clown came into the room.
    ① disappointment　② excitement　　③ harassment　　④ requirement

2. I learned the (　　) story about Pompeii.
    ① fortunate　　② grave　　　③ miserable　　④ tragic

3. Travel in airplane can be (　　) without a book and a smartphone.
    ① astonishing　② dull　　　③ reluctant　　④ vulnerable

4. With many kinds of exercise machines, there's no need to repeat the same routine (　　).
    ① all at once　② day after day　③ day by day　④ one by one

5. We can never be (　　) careful in driving.
    ① so　　　② to　　　③ too　　　④ very

✍ **Production (Write)**　自分の考えを書いて伝えよう【思考力・判断力・表現力】

Write your answer to the following question. (7点)

What would you discuss all afternoon with Ms. Carlyle?

　アドバイス　例えば自分の祖父母と話すことを考えてみよう。

105

"That's rather a big order / to fill, / Peter. // I've seen both plays / but many years ago. // I'll have to read / this evening / and tomorrow morning, / too. // I'm sure / we have a **volume** of Shakespeare / in the house / somewhere. // Well, / you go along home / now, / Peter, / so I can get started. // I've a lot of reading / to do!" //

"But / Ms. Carlyle, / is that all? // Don't you have other things / for me / to do? // Won't there be letters / to write? // Business / to take care of? // People / to telephone? // Shopping / to do?" //

"I have only a few letters / to write / and am still able to write them. // I have a daughter / to take care of my business / and make my phone calls. // There are servants / to do the shopping. // You're going to be here / for one reason, / Peter / — to keep my company. // Don't worry, / my boy! // You'll be enough / with that!" //

That evening, / over a cup of tea / with his friend, / Anne, / he described / what had happened / that afternoon. // "I don't know / what I've got into," / he said, / laughing. //

"It sounds exciting / to me," / Anne told him. // "I think / I'd like Ms. Carlyle. // You're going to have to spend / a lot of time preparing, / though." //

And he did. // The afternoons with Ms. Carlyle / discussing English Literature / helped him as much as any lecture / he heard / at the university, / but he worked hard. // In their discussions / Ms. Carlyle insisted on good reasons / with complete **details**; / she was not satisfied / with half-answers. // Peter often read far into the night / in order to be able to give proper replies / to her questions. // Perhaps, / he thought / as he sat / one evening / reading about the times of Richard III, / this is how teaching will be. // There would be a lot of work / to do, / he decided, / but / if all his students were as interested as Ms. Carlyle / he was going to like it. //

(316 words)

◀)) 音読しよう　　　　　　　　　　　　　　　　　　　スピーキング・トレーナー
Practice 1　スラッシュ位置で文を区切って読んでみよう ☐
Practice 2　音声を聞きながら，音声のすぐ後を追って読んでみよう ☐
TRY!　　　3分10秒以内に本文全体を音読しよう ☐

📖 **Reading**　本文の内容を読んで理解しよう【知識・技能】【思考力・判断力・表現力】　　　共通テスト

Make the correct choice to complete each sentence or answer each question. (各6点)

1. What is the reason that Peter was going to be with Ms. Carlyle? ☐
   ① To do the shopping.　　　② To keep her company.
   ③ To take care of business.　④ To write letters.

2. Anne, Peter's friend, thought ⬚.

① the job sounded boring and she wouldn't like Ms. Carlyle

② the job was exciting and she would like Ms. Carlyle

③ the job was exciting and she would take the job instead of Peter

④ the job was exciting and she wouldn't like Ms. Carlyle

3. Which of the following is true about the discussions with Ms. Carlyle? ⬚

① For Peter, they were much more helpful than the lecture at the university.

② They were very different from what Ms. Carlyle had expected.

③ They were often canceled as Peter had to read far into the night.

④ They were too hard for Ms. Carlyle to catch up with.

🔍 Vocabulary　重要表現について理解しよう【知識】　　　　　　　英検® GTEC®

Make the correct choice to complete each sentence. (各3点)

1. The police recorded every (　　　) they saw at the crime site.

① component　　　② detail　　　③ factor　　　④ total

2. That company is rapidly increasing its sales because its customers are (　　　) with the quality of its products.

① classified　　　② qualified　　　③ satisfied　　　④ unidentified

3. The first (　　　) contains a summary of their research.

① album　　　② novel　　　③ track　　　④ volume

4. The dog went next to her and kept her (　　　) until she stopped crying.

① company　　　② distance　　　③ eyes　　　④ place

5. We spent a lot of time (　　　) a plan for our school trip to Kyoto.

① discuss　　　② discussing　　　③ for discuss　　　④ to discuss

✐ Production (Write)　自分の考えを書いて伝えよう【思考力・判断力・表現力】

Write your answer to the following question. (7点)

Have you ever spent a lot of time preparing something?

アドバイス　修学旅行の計画, 体育祭や文化祭などのような, 共同作業を伴う学校行事について書くのもよいでしょう。

-------------------.--

The following spring / Peter Brent finished his studies / and graduated / from the university, / with honors. // There was Ms. Carlyle / to thank for much / of it. // He never would have done / so well, / had she not made him study. //

The day before he was to leave the university / Peter went to say good-bye / to Ms. Carlyle, / now his very good friend. //

"I will miss you, / Peter," / she told him. // "These hours with you / each afternoon / have been wonderful. // I shall never forget them." //

"But / there'll be more, / Ms. Carlyle. // I'll be teaching / in a school / only five miles / from here / and to come and see you / from time to time / will be no problem / at all." //

"I know, / and I am glad. // It won't be quite the same / but it will be nice / to see you / whenever you can come. // Well, / do you know someone / who can take your place? // I don't intend / to stop my studies / now, / you know. // There's still too much / to learn." //

Peter smiled. // "Is it all right / if it's a woman?" / he asked. //

"Does she know her Literature / as well as you do?" //

"Perhaps / better." // Peter's face suddenly turned red. //

"But / then / I should tell you / that I plan to marry her / when she finishes her studies / next year. // Her name is Anne Eaton." //

"That's good enough / for me." // Ms. Carlyle turned / and pointed to a small box / on the table. // "Oh, / I almost forgot. // That's for you / — a graduation present." //

The young man picked up the box / and opened it. // Inside was a gold watch. //

"It was Arthur's," / the old lady said / softly, / "and I want you / to have it. // When you look at the time / perhaps you'll remember me / and the happy hours / we've spent here / together, / you, / the great writers / and I." //

Peter looked at the watch / a long time. // Then, / turning / and smiling at the old lady / in the wheelchair, / he leaned over / and kissed her / on the **forehead**. // "Most of all, / I'll have memories / of you," / he said. //　(388 words)

 音読しよう　　　　　　　　　　　　　　　　　　　スピーキング・トレーナー

Practice 1　スラッシュ位置で文を区切って読んでみよう □
Practice 2　音声を聞きながら，音声のすぐ後を追って読んでみよう □
TRY!　　　　3分50秒以内に本文全体を音読しよう □

📖 **Reading**　本文の内容を読んで理解しよう【知識・技能】【思考力・判断力・表現力】　　共通テスト

Make the correct choice to complete each sentence or answer each question. (各6点)

1. What does "graduated … with honors" in line 1 mean? ☐
   ① Graduated by receiving rewards　　② Graduated with academic colleagues
   ③ Graduated with feeling of proud　　④ Graduated with high achievement

2. When talking about Peter's replacement with Ms. Carlyle, his face suddenly turned red because ☐.
   ① he didn't know what the woman's major was
   ② he had to admit the woman knew about literature better than him
   ③ he knew that Ms. Carlyle preferred men to women
   ④ he was going to tell Ms. Carlyle about his fiancée

3. What was supposedly the best present Peter got from Ms. Carlyle? ☐
   ① A kiss on his forehead.　　② Arthur's gold watch.
   ③ Books of the great writers.　　④ Memories of his time with Ms. Carlyle.

🔍 **Vocabulary**　重要表現について理解しよう【知識】　　英検 ® GTEC®

Make the correct choice to complete each sentence. (各3点)

1. Oh, it's midnight already!? I spent more than I (　　) to.
   ① created　　② intended　　③ supposed　　④ strived

2. The walls of the wooden house were (　　) over from the force of the winds.
   ① declining　　② leaning　　③ reclining　　④ tending

3. Whenever the church clock's hands (　　) to twelve, I hear the bells.
   ① announce　　② finish　　③ point　　④ sign

4. The boundaries between the two tribes have varied from (　　).
   ① head to toe　　② now on　　③ time to time　　④ that time on

5. (　　) you be unable to visit us, call me in advance.
   ① Could　　② Did　　③ Should　　④ Were

✐ **Production (Write)**　自分の考えを書いて伝えよう【思考力・判断力・表現力】

Write your answer to the following question. (7点)

What is the best gift you've ever received?

アドバイス　友達や家族からもらった贈り物について，なぜそれが一番なのかの理由も付け加えて記述したい。

Jake Belknap found an old desk / in a **secondhand** store / near his **apartment** / one Saturday afternoon. // The desk came / from an old house / built in the middle of the nineteenth century / in Brooklyn. //

I never wondered / or cared / who might have used it / long ago. // I bought it / because it was cheap. //

I'm twenty-four years old, / and I live in Brooklyn / and work in Manhattan. // I bring work home / from the office / once in a while. // And every couple of weeks / or so / I write a letter / to my folks / in Florida. // So I'd been needing a desk. //

The desk was made of heavy wood. // At the back of it / rose little **compartments** / about two feet / above the **desktop**. // **Underneath** them / was a row of three little **drawers**. //

On that night, / after working for a while / at the desk, / I pulled out one of the drawers / and held it up / in my hand, / **admiring** its construction. // And then / it suddenly occurred / to me / that the little drawer / in my hand / was only six inches deep, / while the top of the desk extended / at least / a foot back. //

I pushed my hand / into the opening / and could feel the handle / of a secret drawer / hidden in the back. // I pulled it out. //

There was some plain white writing paper, / three or four blank **envelopes**, / a small round glass bottle / of ink, / and a plain black wooden pen. // I saw / that one of the envelopes was slightly thicker / than the others. // I opened it / and found a letter / inside. // Even before I saw the date, / I knew / this letter was *old*. // The **handwriting** was beautifully clear, / the letters **elegant** and perfectly formed. // The ink was **rust**-black, / the date / at the top of the page was May 14, 1882, / and reading it, / I saw that it was a love letter. // It began: //

Dearest! //

Mother, / Father, / and Willy / have long since **retired** to sleep. // Now, / the night far advanced, / the house silent, / I alone remain awake, / at last free to speak / to you / as I choose. // Yes, / I am **willing** to say it! // I long for the **tender warmth** / of your look! // (325 words)

🔊 音読しよう
Practice 1　スラッシュ位置で文を区切って読んでみよう □
Practice 2　音声を聞きながら，音声のすぐ後を追って読んでみよう □
TRY!　　　　3分20秒以内に本文全体を音読しよう □

スピーキング・トレーナー

📖 Reading　本文の内容を読んで理解しよう【知識・技能】【思考力・判断力・表現力】　　共通テスト

Make the correct choice to complete each sentence or answer each question. (各6点)

1. What does "folks" in line 8 mean? ☐

   ① colleagues　　　② people　　　③ neighbors　　　④ parents

2. Which of the following is true about the desk? ☐

   ① It had little compartments underneath a row of three little drawers.

   ② It had a secret drawer hidden in the back of a front drawer.

   ③ It was made in the middle of the nineteenth century in Brooklyn.

   ④ It was sold in a secondhand store at a high price.

3. Which of the following was **not** contained in the secret drawer? ☐

   ① A plain black feather pen.　　　② A small round glass bottle of ink.

   ③ Some plain white writing paper.　　④ Three or four blank envelopes.

🔍 Vocabulary　重要表現について理解しよう【知識】　　英検® GTEC®

Make the correct choice to complete each sentence. (各3点)

1. The Great *Torii*, the symbol of Miyajima, which we (　　　　), was first built in the 12th century.

   ① admire　　　② criticize　　　③ help　　　④ recommend

2. It never occurred (　　　) him to call the police for help.

   ① at　　　② in　　　③ on　　　④ to

3. Half of the members of the House of Councilors (　　　) every three years.

   ① dismiss　　　② retire　　　③ shrink　　　④ withdraw

4. People all over the world have (　　　　) for peace.

   ① desired　　　② insisted　　　③ longed　　　④ requested

5. A wolf blew down the two pigs' houses which were made (　　　　) straw and sticks.

   ① by　　　② from　　　③ of　　　④ with

✏️ Production（Write）　自分の考えを書いて伝えよう【思考力・判断力・表現力】

Write your answer to the following question. (7点)

Have you ever bought anything from a secondhand shop?

> **アドバイス**　中古店での経験や，フリーマーケットでの買い物の経験などでもよいでしょう。買った物の説明なども付け加えたい。

I smiled a little. // People once expressed themselves / using **elaborate** phrases / like these. // But I wondered / why it had never been sent. //

Dear one: / I have to marry a man / I do not love. // To please my father / I have tried / and sadly I know / I have the duty / to **obey** / and must **accept** soon. //

If only you could save me / from that! // But you cannot / — for you exist only in my mind. // But / though you live only in my **imagination**, / and though I shall never see your like, / you are more dear to me / than the man / to whom I am engaged. //

I think of you / constantly. // I dream of you. // I speak with you / — in my mind and heart. // If only you existed / outside them! // **Sweetheart**, / good night. // Dream of me, / too. //

With all my love, / I am, //

your Helen //

At the bottom of the page / was written, / "Miss Helen Elizabeth Worley, / 972 Brock Place, / Brooklyn, / New York." //

I was no longer smiling / at this cry / from the heart / in the middle of a long-ago night. // As I read her words, / she seemed alive / and real to me. // And my heart went out / to her / as I stared down at her secret, / **hopeless** appeal / against the world and time / she lived in. //

I don't know why, / but in the silence / of that spring night, / it seemed natural enough / to remove the **cork** / from the old bottle of ink, / pick up the pen beside it, / and then, / spreading a sheet of yellowing old **notepaper** / on the desk, / to begin to write. // I felt / that I was communicating / with a still-living young woman / when I wrote: //

Helen: //

I have just read the letter / in the secret drawer / of your desk. // I can't tell / what you might think of me / if there were a way / I could reach you. // Do the best you can, / Helen Elizabeth Worley, / in the time and place / you are. // I can't reach you / or help you. // But I'll think of you. // And maybe I'll dream of you, / too. //

Yours, /

Jake Belknap // (347 words)

🔊 **音読しよう**　　　　　　　　　　　　　　　　　　　　　スピーキング・トレーナー

Practice 1　スラッシュ位置で文を区切って読んでみよう ☐
Practice 2　音声を聞きながら，音声のすぐ後を追って読んでみよう ☐
TRY!　　　3分30秒以内に本文全体を音読しよう ☐

📖 Reading　本文の内容を読んで理解しよう【知識・技能】【思考力・判断力・表現力】　　　共通テスト

Make the correct choice to complete each sentence or answer each question. (各9点)

1. Choose the correct answer to the question "why it had never been sent" in line 2.

   ① Because the letter was for a person who didn't exist.
   ② Because Helen left it in the secret drawer and forgot about it.
   ③ Because Helen got married before sending it.
   ④ Because Helen's father didn't allow her to do it.

2. After reading the letter, Jake stopped smiling because ⬚.
   ① he found it strange that she would write a letter to an imaginary lover
   ② he knew her hopeless cry and felt pity for her
   ③ he began to feel guilty about reading her letter
   ④ he was astonished with the beautifully written letter

🔍 Vocabulary　重要表現について理解しよう【知識】　　　英検® GTEC®

Make the correct choice to complete each sentence. (各3点)

1. He was talking to a girl that every boy his age would dream (　　　).
   ① about　　　② in　　　③ of　　　④ with

2. Catherine, who was (　　　) to Peter III, moved to Russia when she was 16.
   ① committed　　② employed　　③ engaged　　④ pledged

3. More and more tourists are visiting the area but some stores still don't (　　　) e-money.
   ① accept　　② allow　　③ approve　　④ assume

4. My dog never (　　　) my words, only my father's.
   ① achieves　　② differs　　③ obeys　　④ regards

5. If only I (　　　) lost his address. He must think I'm rude for not contacting him.
   ① didn't　　② hadn't　　③ haven't　　④ wouldn't

✏️ Production (Write)　自分の考えを書いて伝えよう【思考力・判断力・表現力】

Write your answer to the following question. (7点)

Have you kept a diary?

アドバイス　日記をつけたことがあれば，つけた頻度や，どのようなことを書いていたかについて書いてみよう。つけたことがない場合は，つけることを想像して書いてみよう。

Maybe / what I did seems **foolish**. // It's hard to explain. // Still, / I **folded** the paper, / put it / into one of the old envelopes, / and sealed it. // Then / I wrote / "Ms. Helen Worley" / and her address / on the face of the envelope. // I put an old stamp / on it, / picked it up, / and walked out of my apartment / into the darkness of the night, / heading for the Wister Post Office, / one of the oldest post offices / in Brooklyn, / built, / I suppose, / not much after the Civil War. //

I was extremely busy / all the next week. // That Friday evening / I worked at home, / sitting at my desk. // But once more now, / Helen Elizabeth Worley was in my mind. // I worked **steadily** / all evening, / and it was around twelve-thirty / when I finished. // I opened the little center drawer of the desk / into which I'd put some **rubber** bands / and paper clips. // And then / I realized / suddenly / that *it* too, / of course, / must have a secret drawer / behind it. //

I hadn't thought of that. // It simply hadn't occurred to me / the week before. // And I'd been too busy all week / to think of it / since. // But now / I pulled the center drawer / all the way out, / reached in, / and touched the little handle there. // I pulled out the second secret drawer / and there / I found another letter / in rust-black ink / on yellowing old paper. // It read: //

Please, / oh, / please / — who are you? // Where can I reach you? // Your letter arrived / today. // I cannot **conceive** / how you saw my letter / in its secret place, / but since you did, / perhaps you will see this one / too. // Oh, / tell me / your letter is no trick / or **cruel** joke! // If I now address someone / who has truly responded / to my most secret hopes / — do not for a moment longer keep me **ignorant** / of who and where you are. //

I must hear from you / again. // I shall not rest / until I do. //

I remain, / most sincerely, /

Helen Elizabeth Worley // (332 words)

🔊 音読しよう   スピーキング・トレーナー

Practice 1   スラッシュ位置で文を区切って読んでみよう ☐
Practice 2   音声を聞きながら，音声のすぐ後を追って読んでみよう ☐
TRY!   3分20秒以内に本文全体を音読しよう ☐

📖 Reading 　本文の内容を読んで理解しよう【知識・技能】【思考力・判断力・表現力】 　共通テスト

Make the correct choice to complete each sentence or answer each question. (各6点)

1. Put the events in the order that Jake did. ☐ → ☐ → ☐ → ☐ → ☐

   ① Jake found another letter in the second secret drawer.

   ② Jake headed for the Wister Post Office with a letter.

   ③ Jake put an old stamp on the envelope.

   ④ Jake spent an extremely busy week.

   ⑤ Jake wrote Helen's name and address on the envelope.

2. What does "head for" mean in line 5? ☐

   ① follow behind ② go toward ③ move back to ④ turn around

3. In Helen's second letter, she expressed her desire to ☐.

   ① be saved from her unwilling marriage

   ② get the answer to the trick

   ③ hear from the stranger more often

   ④ know who wrote to her and where that person was

🔍 Vocabulary 　重要表現について理解しよう【知識】 　英検® GTEC®

Make the correct choice to complete each sentence. (各3点)

1. It is said that John (　　　) the idea of the lyrics when watching the news of war.

   ① conceived ② doubted ③ invented ④ reflected

2. We are so pleased to (　　　) you!

   ① catch up ② hear from ③ keep in touch ④ write to

3. They struggled to end the long-lasting and (　　　) war.

   ① benevolent ② crucial ③ cruel ④ merciful

4. The government treated its people like (　　　) children.

   ① expert ② fond ③ ignorant ④ relieved

5. He had long regretted losing the game because of a (　　　) mistake.

   ① bright ② foolish ③ linear ④ perfect

✍ Production (Write) 　自分の考えを書いて伝えよう【思考力・判断力・表現力】

Write your answer to the following question. (7点)

When was the last time you wrote to someone?

アドバイス　だれ宛てで，どんな内容だったか，思い出して書いてみよう。メールでもいいでしょう。

After a long time, / I opened the first little drawer / of the old desk, / and took out the pen and ink / I'd found there / and a sheet of the notepaper. //

For minutes, / with the pen in my hand, / I sat there / staring down at the empty paper. // Finally, / I **dipped** the pen into the old ink / and wrote: //

Helen, / my dear: //

I don't know / how to say this, / but I do exist, / here / in Brooklyn, / less than three blocks / from where you now read this / — in the year 1994. // We are separated / not by space / but by the years / that lie between us. // Now / I own the desk / that you once had / and at which you wrote the note I found / in it. // Helen, / all I can tell you is / that I answered that note, / mailed it / late at night / at the old Wister Post Office, / and that it somehow reached you, / as I hope / this will too. //

This is no trick! // Can you imagine anyone playing a trick / that cruel? // You must believe me. // I live. // I exist, / 112 years after you read this, / and with the feeling / that I have fallen in love / with you. //

I sat for some time / staring at the wall, / trying to figure out / how to explain something / I was certain / was true. // Then / I wrote: //

Helen: // There are three secret drawers / in our desk. // Into the first / you put only the letter / I found. // Nothing else can now come down to me / in that drawer, / for you cannot now **alter** / what you have already done. //

Into the second drawer, / you put the note / that lies before me, / which I found / when I opened the drawer / a few minutes ago. // You put nothing else into it, / and now that, / too, / cannot be changed. //

But / I haven't opened the third drawer, / Helen. // Not yet! // It is the last way / you can still reach me, / and the last time. // I will mail this / as I did before, / then wait. // In a week / I will open the last drawer. //

Jake Belknap // (345 words)

🔊 音読しよう

Practice 1 スラッシュ位置で文を区切って読んでみよう ☐

Practice 2 音声を聞きながら，音声のすぐ後を追って読んでみよう ☐

TRY! 3分30秒以内に本文全体を音読しよう ☐

スピーキング・トレーナー

📖 Reading　本文の内容を読んで理解しよう【知識・技能】【思考力・判断力・表現力】　　共通テスト

Make the correct choice to complete each sentence or answer each question. (各6点)

1. According to Jake, what separated Helen and him? ☐

   ① Helen's parents　　② The desk　　　　③ The distance　　　④ The years

2. While writing to Helen, Jake sat for a while staring at the wall because he ☐.

   ① couldn't figure out how to explain to her what was going to happen

   ② couldn't stop feeling love for Helen

   ③ was not sure if what he thought was true

   ④ was thinking about what trick he was going to play on her

3. When was Jake going to open the third drawer? ☐

   ① After he finish writing the letter　　② Never

   ③ One week later　　　　　　　　　　④ The next day

🔍 Vocabulary　重要表現について理解しよう【知識】　　英検® GTEC®

Make the correct choice to complete each sentence. (各3点)

1. The boys planned to play a (　　　) on their new teacher.

   ① game　　　　　② practice　　　　　③ secret　　　　　④ trick

2. Her first essay was so perfect that the critics would be impossible to (　　　) a single word for the better.

   ① alter　　　　　② revisit　　　　　③ transform　　　　④ vary

3. After coating with flour, (　　　) the pork into beaten eggs.

   ① dip　　　　　② drop　　　　　③ fill　　　　　④ moisten

4. We decided to stay at home, (　　　) heavy rain was expected.

   ① for　　　　　② no　　　　　③ so　　　　　④ till

5. (　　　) she has grown up, it's time for her to help those who need this place.

   ① As soon as　　② In case　　　③ Now that　　　④ Unless

✍ Production (Write)　自分の考えを書いて伝えよう【思考力・判断力・表現力】

Write your answer to the following question. (7点)

　　Have you ever played a trick on somebody?

　　アドバイス　経験を描写するか，経験がない理由を説明しよう。

It was a long week. // I was terribly **tempted** / to open the third secret drawer earlier, / but I wasn't sure, / and I waited. //

Then, / late at night, / a week to the hour / after I'd mailed my second letter / at the old Wister Post Office, / I pulled it out. // I'd expected a very long letter, / of many pages, / and full of everything / she wanted to say. // But there was no letter / at all. // There was only a photograph, / about three inches square, / faded brown in color. //   The photograph showed a beautiful young woman / in a high-necked dark dress. //

Across the bottom of her photograph / she had written, / "I shall never forget you." // And as I sat there / at the old desk, / staring at / what she had written, / I understood that, / of course / that was the last time, / as she knew, / that she'd ever be able to reach me. //

It wasn't the last time, / though. // There was one final way / for Helen Worley / to communicate with me / over the years, / and it took me / a long time, / as it must have taken her, / to realize it. //

Only a week ago, / after much searching, / I finally found it. // I found the old **headstone** / in the **cemetery**, / among the others stretching off / in rows / under the quiet trees. // And then / I read the **inscription** / carved into the weathered old stone: / *Helen Elizabeth Worley* / —— *1861-1934.* // Under this / were the words, / "I NEVER FORGOT." //

And neither will I. //   (243 words)

 音読しよう

スピーキング・トレーナー

Practice 1   スラッシュ位置で文を区切って読んでみよう ☐
Practice 2   音声を聞きながら，音声のすぐ後を追って読んでみよう ☐
TRY!   2分30秒以内に本文全体を音読しよう ☐

◀) シャドーイングをすることができる。　　　　　　　　　📖 Part 5を読んで概要や要点を捉えることができる。
🔍 文脈を理解して適切な語句を用いて英文を完成することができる。
✐ 自分の墓石にどのような内容の碑文を刻むかについて簡単な語句を用いて考えを表現することができる。

Goals

📖 Reading　本文の内容を読んで理解しよう【知識・技能】【思考力・判断力・表現力】　共通テスト

Make the correct choice to answer each question. (各6点)

1. Why did Jake wait a week before opening the third secret drawer? ☐
   ① Because he wanted to see if the drawer would open on its own.
   ② Because he was afraid of what he might find inside.
   ③ Because he was too busy to open it earlier.
   ④ Because he was unsure whether it was the right time to open it.

2. What did Jake expect to find in the third drawer? ☐
   ① A handle to another secret drawer.　　② A pen and notepaper.
   ③ A photograph.　　④ A very long letter of many pages.

3. What was the last way Helen used to communicate with Jake? ☐
   ① Her headstone inscriptions.　　② Her inscriptions on the desk.
   ③ Her note on yellowing paper.　　④ Her photograph in the third drawer.

🔍 Vocabulary　重要表現について理解しよう【知識】　英検 GTEC

Make the correct choice to complete each sentence. (各3点)

1. My uncle gave us the address of the (　　　) where our family member is buried.
   ① cemetery　　② ground　　③ mound　　④ tombstone

2. I looked at the (　　　) on the gravestones and wondered about their lives.
   ① descriptions　　② inscriptions　　③ prescriptions　　④ subscriptions

3. In an afternoon like this, I am (　　　) to leave school and dive into a pool.
   ① caught　　② driven　　③ led　　④ tempted

4. The oldest (　　　) in the graveyard shows the date of 1810.
   ① advertisement　　② bible　　③ headstone　　④ title

5. My mother usually doesn't stay up late, and (　　　).
   ① my father does neither　　② my father does so
   ③ neither does my father　　④ so does my father

✐ Production (Write)　自分の考えを書いて伝えよう【思考力・判断力・表現力】

Write your answer to the following question. (7点)

What would you like to inscribe in your headstone?

アドバイス　まだまだ遠い先のことではあるが，これまでの自分の生活をよく思い返して想像して書いてみよう。

WPM・得点一覧表

●スピーキング・トレーナーを使って，各レッスンの本文を流暢に音読できるようにしましょう。下の計算式を使って，1分あたりに音読できた語数（words per minute）を算出してみましょう。

【本文の総語数】÷【音読にかかった時間(秒)】×60
= [   ] wpm

Preparatory		WPM	得点
1	CHECK	/ wpm	/ 40
	TRY	/ wpm	/ 40
2	CHECK	/ wpm	/ 40
	TRY	/ wpm	/ 40
3	CHECK	/ wpm	/ 40
	TRY	/ wpm	/ 40
	流暢さの目安	100 wpm	/ 240

Lesson		WPM	得点
1	1～3	/ wpm	/ 40
	4～6	/ wpm	/ 40
	7～9	/ wpm	/ 40
	AP	/ wpm	/ 40
	流暢さの目安	100 wpm	/ 160

Lesson		WPM	得点
2	1～3	/ wpm	/ 40
	4～6	/ wpm	/ 40
	7～9	/ wpm	/ 40
	AP	/ wpm	/ 40
	流暢さの目安	100 wpm	/ 160

Lesson		WPM	得点
3	1～3	/ wpm	/ 40
	4～6	/ wpm	/ 40
	7～9	/ wpm	/ 40
	AP	/ wpm	/ 40
	流暢さの目安	100 wpm	/ 160

Lesson		WPM	得点
4	1～3	/ wpm	/ 40
	4～6	/ wpm	/ 40
	7～9	/ wpm	/ 40
	AP	/ wpm	/ 40
	流暢さの目安	100 wpm	/ 160

Lesson		WPM	得点
5	1～3	/ wpm	/ 40
	4～6	/ wpm	/ 40
	7～9	/ wpm	/ 40
	AP	/ wpm	/ 40
	流暢さの目安	100 wpm	/ 160

Lesson		WPM	得点
6	1～3	/ wpm	/ 40
	4～6	/ wpm	/ 40
	7～9	/ wpm	/ 40
	AP	/ wpm	/ 40
	流暢さの目安	100 wpm	/ 160

Lesson		WPM	得点
7	1～3	/ wpm	/ 40
	4～6	/ wpm	/ 40
	7～9	/ wpm	/ 40
	AP	/ wpm	/ 40
	流暢さの目安	100 wpm	/ 160

Lesson		WPM	得点
8	1～3	/ wpm	/ 40
	4～6	/ wpm	/ 40
	7～9	/ wpm	/ 40
	AP	/ wpm	/ 40
	流暢さの目安	100 wpm	/ 160

Lesson		WPM	得点
9	1～3	/ wpm	/ 40
	4～6	/ wpm	/ 40
	7～9	/ wpm	/ 40
	10～12	/ wpm	/ 40
	AP	/ wpm	/ 40
	流暢さの目安	100 wpm	/ 200

Lesson		WPM	得点
10	1～3	/ wpm	/ 40
	4～6	/ wpm	/ 40
	7～9	/ wpm	/ 40
	10～12	/ wpm	/ 40
	AP	/ wpm	/ 40
	流暢さの目安	100 wpm	/ 200

Optional		WPM	得点
1	Part 1	/ wpm	/ 40
	Part 2	/ wpm	/ 40
	Part 3	/ wpm	/ 40
	Part 4	/ wpm	/ 40
	Part 5	/ wpm	/ 40
	流暢さの目安	100 wpm	/ 200

Optional		WPM	得点
2	Part 1	/ wpm	/ 40
	Part 2	/ wpm	/ 40
	Part 3	/ wpm	/ 40
	Part 4	/ wpm	/ 40
	Part 5	/ wpm	/ 40
	流暢さの目安	100 wpm	/ 200